P9-CQY-813

Life and Thought in the Early Middle Ages

THE CHAPTERS of this volume originated as
public lectures given by the authors in the annual Spring Lecture Series, 1963, sponsored by
the General Extension Division of the
University of Minnesota

LIFE AND THOUGHT
in the
EARLY MIDDLE AGES

⟩ EDITED BY ROBERT S. HOYT ⟨

The University of Minnesota Press
MINNEAPOLIS

WINGATE COLLEGE LIBRARY
WINGATE N C

© Copyright 1967 by the University of Minnesota. All rights reserved

Printed in the United States of America at the
Lund Press, Minneapolis

Library of Congress Catalog Card Number : 67-15065

PUBLISHED IN GREAT BRITAIN, INDIA, AND PAKISTAN BY THE OXFORD
UNIVERSITY PRESS, LONDON, BOMBAY, AND KARACHI, AND IN CANADA
BY THE COPP CLARK PUBLISHING CO. LIMITED, TORONTO

CONTENTS

37887

Life and Thought in the Early Middle Ages

} ROBERT S. HOYT {

INTRODUCTION

THE period covered by the essays in this volume extends from the establishment of the Germanic "successor states" in the western provinces of the Roman Empire to the appearance of some of the economic and feudal institutions that were to provide a basis for the civilization of the high Middle Ages. It is the period once commonly called "the Dark Ages." In modern medieval scholarship the label is no longer used because its implications are rejected. The early medieval period was "dark" to an earlier generation of historians because it was barbaric, decadent, backward, undeveloped, and characterized by an absence of the arts and letters, the economic prosperity, the political order, and above all the unity enjoyed by the ancient world under the *Pax Romana*. Early medieval Europe was not only barbaric, it was a fragmented and localized world. Even where glimmers of light could be discerned, they illumined only one or another corner of a world generally obscured by gloom.

A historical period that produces little written evidence, in the form either of literature or of records, is "dark" because its culture is relatively undeveloped; conversely, it is dark in the sense that historians know little about it because there is so little surviving evidence. But this generalization has much less force today than,

3

say, in the second half of the nineteenth century, even though the total evidence available to the historian today is not significantly greater than a hundred years earlier. New evidence of whatever sort, whether textual or archaeological, has done much less to advance historical knowledge of the period than the development of critical scholarship. Almost all of the texts available now were known a century ago, but most of them were not yet critically edited and their meaning and significance were less certain than now. The advance in historical knowledge has been primarily qualitative; but this qualitative advance has also produced a quantitative increase in knowledge, in the sense that many views or interpretations that were hitherto speculative or impressionistic may now be considered either firmly established or at least better founded on a critical understanding of what evidence has survived. It is not surprising that as more has become known, and known more certainly, about the early medieval period, historians have given up the label "dark," with its pejorative implications.

The term originated as an epithet to stigmatize all the centuries that lay between the conversion of Constantine and the early fourteenth century, when classical Latin belles-lettres began to be cultivated and imitated by the early humanists. But even the humanists could distinguish between the greater darkness of the earlier centuries and the lesser darkness of the later centuries during which the city-states in Italy achieved some measure of political liberty. What the humanists saw dimly the historians of the early twentieth century spelled out clearly in terms of "the renaissance of the twelfth century" or of the culmination of a distinct medieval civilization that flowered in the high Middle Ages (c. 1050–1300).

This recognition of the importance of, and enduring contribution to Western civilization of, the high Middle Ages led inevitably (and logically) to a re-evaluation of the preceding period, the centuries intervening between the decline of antiquity and the high Middle Ages. This early medieval period could not be wholly "dark" or hopelessly barbaric and devoid of historical significance, or else the renaissance of the twelfth century could not be explained. That renaissance was above all distinct from and not simply a resumption of classical civilization, although the label itself connotes a rebirth or recovery of classical elements as vital ingredients in medieval culture. The early medieval period could only have been relatively "dark," for if all was totally "dark" in the period a renaissance could hardly have begun in the mid-eleventh century. If the centuries following the Roman Empire were an aftermath of a higher civilization, they were also the prelude to another higher civilization — as well as a connecting link between the classical elements common to each. These centuries, from the fourth to the eleventh, constitute a long period during which new and distinctively medieval elements appeared and developed. There must therefore have been vitality and novelty as well as decline, barbarism, and darkness in the early medieval period.

The essays in this volume illustrate, as they contribute to our knowledge of, several aspects of the early Middle Ages. More basically, they also illustrate the view — held by the majority of medieval historians today — that the significance of the period is far better summed up in words like "transition" or "transformation" than by such time-worn and worn-out labels as "the Dark Ages." The emphasis has shifted from decline to difference, and — in properly objective fashion — it has also become common to avoid the value judgments necessarily implied by such terms as "fall" or "barbarism" in much the same way as the terms "monkish" or "popish" have long since, in historical literature, given way to "monastic" and "papal."

Even more important, perhaps, the following essays illustrate the conviction among early medieval historians today that the period must be studied for its own sake and not simply in its relationship to what preceded or followed. What is essentially early medieval, then, must be found not only in elements of continuity either from the Roman past or toward the high medieval future, but more in those elements of change that give the early medieval world its distinctive character and hence its significance in the scheme of periodization that historians have employed in dealing with the origins of Western civilization. Some of these distinctively early medieval elements of change were destructive, some creative or productive, but all worked toward building a new civilization for which the Mediterranean was to be a frontier rather than the center. This new civilization, western and Latin medieval Christendom, was as distinct from antiquity and the modern world as it was from the civilization of the contemporary Byzantine and Moslem worlds. Although the obviously new forces producing this result were the Germanic, Celtic, and other barbarian contributions, these latter cannot be considered in isolation from the Roman and Christian heritage from antiquity. The main themes of the formative early Middle Ages were assimilation and synthesis of the Roman, the Christian, and the barbarian elements; until assimilation and synthesis were achieved, no medieval civilization could emerge and flourish. The authors of this volume have each dealt with a specific aspect of the whole process, and no attempt has been made (nor could it be made in a volume of this compass) to deal in comparable detail with all aspects of early medieval history.

} KATHERINE FISCHER DREW {

THE BARBARIAN KINGS
AS LAWGIVERS AND JUDGES

WE KNOW relatively little about the organization of the Germanic
barbarian tribes before they entered the Roman Empire. The Germans themselves left no records of this period of their history, and
it is only in references to these people in the works of a number of
Roman and Byzantine writers that such information as we have is
found.

There is some reason to believe that the institution of kingship
was not well developed among the Germans before their entry into
the territory of the Roman Empire. Caesar seems to have thought
that the Germanic tribes did not ordinarily have kings in the first
century B.C. but that leadership, political and judicial, was offered
by *principes* who directed small divisional groups within the larger
tribe. Tacitus, writing some one hundred and fifty years later, implied that the institution of kingship was more common and that
tribal kings were selected on the basis of their noble birth. Occasionally, those tribes which already had kings might select special
war leaders, or *duces*, whose authority superseded that of the king
for the duration of the military emergency.

Unfortunately, our knowledge of the pre-conquest Germanic

7

kingship rests upon what is, after all, inadequate evidence. We are on surer ground for the period beginning with the major invasions of the fifth century. With one or two notable exceptions, our sources now are no longer Roman commentators but the products of the Germanic kingship itself: a number of law codes issued by the Germanic kings for their own people and for the Roman provincials under their domination.

With the possible exception of the Anglo-Saxons, all the Germanic invaders of the Empire in the fifth and sixth centuries entered under the leadership of tribal kings such as Alaric the Visigoth, Theodoric the Ostrogoth, Gundobad the Burgundian, and Alboin the Lombard. There is no doubt that each of these kings had the support of his people and each had a claim to royalty based on more than simply election or immediate military necessity. All were members of recognized royal dynasties of rulers, even if their elevation had been confirmed by formal election or designation by the warriors of their nation.

It is hard to distinguish between the military and political functions of these early Germanic rulers. Once across the Roman frontier, most of the Germanic invaders in the fifth century managed to establish a *modus vivendi* with the Empire whereby the barbarians were ceded lands for settlement in return for the promise of military service to Rome. Accordingly, the Germanic kings found themselves immediately faced with the problem of regulating the division of lands between their followers and the Roman hosts to whom they were assigned, of establishing a government for the territory now occupied by their nation, and of providing an administration which could handle the problems of both Germanic and Roman subjects.

The barbarian tribes that were allowed to settle in the Empire in the fifth century usually created nominally dependent kingdoms within the framework of the weakened western Roman Empire. Technically, the Germans were *foederati* or military allies of the Empire, although in actual fact the barbarians had established kingdoms which were for all practical purposes independent of Roman control. Barbarian kings now replaced the former Roman provincial governors and fell heir to the administrative duties of these officials.

That the barbarian kings both understood the task facing them and accomplished it with considerable success is strong indication that the Germanic kingship was no new institution. The power of this king may not have been absolute — it may have been limited by the demands of a warrior aristocracy upon whose support the king necessarily relied — but the law codes reveal the king was not only the head of the military forces of the nation but also the head of the administrative and judicial machinery. In adapting themselves and their people to their new condition, the barbarian kings doubtless retained the services of many members of the former provincial administration — here we can recall the services rendered to Theodoric the Ostrogoth by the Romans Boethius and Cassiodorus. Nonetheless, the presence of the barbarians who, in effect, constituted a ruling aristocracy inevitably brought deep-reaching adjustments in the lives and habits of the Roman provincials.

The literate Roman population among which the Germanic barbarians settled was curiously silent about its new neighbors and rulers. With the exception of a few passing remarks about the uncouthness of the Germanic settlers by Salvian, Sidonius Apollinaris, and Cassiodorus, most Roman writers ignored the fact that real power had passed from the hands of Roman provincials into the hands of the Germanic king and his court and continued to describe their own private routine and their travels from one villa to another.

Even though the Roman provincials tried to ignore the barbarians as much as possible, it was inevitable that the presence of these relatively unsophisticated Germans within the Empire would produce a cultural decline among the Roman inhabitants and an uplift in cultural level for the barbarians. Among other results, Roman law felt the effects of invasion. There was a marked deterioration in legal reasoning during the fifth and sixth centuries as the vast bulk of Roman law became unusable by both Roman and barbarian judges in the barbarian kingdoms. Even such compilations as the fifth-century *Theodosian Code* were too sophisticated for their less complex social and economic institutions.

But the barbarian kings were not hostile to Roman law, just as they were not hostile to Roman culture in general. Their lawgiving activities provide us with some of our most reliable evidence of their sincere attempts to demonstrate the strength of the new Germanic states and their determination to maintain the institutions of old Rome. Of course, the barbarian kings could not actually maintain all the institutions of old Rome in the field of law, but they made surprisingly significant steps in this direction.

The legal activities of the Germanic barbarian kings have been noted by many legal historians and the barbarian codes have been studied in considerable detail, especially by European scholars. My purpose here is not to offer any significant new interpretation of the legal activities of the barbarian rulers, but rather to present that interpretation which seems most likely to me in the light of my own researches and to offer support for this interpretation from the barbarian codes.

The Germanic barbarians had no written codes of law before their entry into the Roman Empire. As a matter of fact, we know surprisingly little about the early legal institutions of the Germans although we do have some information about their social and political institutions from such Roman writers as Caesar, Tacitus, and Procopius, and we are able to draw some conclusions from the much later legal concepts of those Teutonic peoples who did not enter the Empire and remained out of contact with European civilization in general until approximately the ninth century. As a result of the study of these materials, there is little doubt about the general legal practices of the Germans at the time of the migrations. Their law was essentially customary law — the traditions or customs handed down by word of mouth from untold generations in the past. Such customs were preserved in the minds of the elders of the tribe who on occasion might be called together to speak the law. The king might well be one of these elders, but even if he were, he could not "make" the laws — he could only speak (with the advice of the elders) and say what the custom of the tribe was.

And since Germanic custom prescribed penalty as well as defined offense, the king's legal activities were thus confined to his presiding over the court or council which had met to speak the law.

Once the barbarians had been allowed to settle within the Empire and to establish dependent kingdoms for themselves, the role of the barbarian king developed rapidly. The tribe or nation tended to be spread widely as the barbarians took up vacant lands or shared cultivated fields with their Roman hosts. Under such conditions, the identity of the tribe tended to weaken and the unwritten customs of the people tended to fade or failed to serve the increasingly more complex social and economic institutions of the people.

The barbarians' response to the challenge of Roman culture varied in accordance with the time of their migrations and with the portion of the Empire in which they settled. Those nations which entered the Empire early and settled in the more advanced southern sections encountered a numerous Roman population and a well-established Roman legal culture. As a result, the legislative activities of their kings would reflect considerable influence by Roman law and Roman legal practices. They also reflected genuine concern in administering a well-recognized code of Roman law for the Roman part of the population.

On the other hand, the law codes issued by the rulers of tribes which settled in the more backward northern part of the Roman Empire reflected little if any influence by the Roman law, and the rulers of these northern kingdoms were little concerned about providing a code of Roman law or judges learned in the Roman law for the remnants of the former Roman population in their kingdoms.

In the situation which developed in the southern kingdoms, the Germanic attitude toward law in general provided a rational justification for the legal responsibilities of the barbarian kings in their new position, ruling over native tribesmen and provincial Roman population. The Germans regarded law as a national possession — each nation had its own laws or customs and each member of the tribe possessed this "law" and carried it with him wherever he went. This principle is known as "personality of law" and is in contrast with the idea of territorial law whereby all persons residing in a given state or territory are subject to the same law. If the new Germanic kings but extended their traditional personal-law attitude toward all their subjects, both Germanic and Roman, then each people might continue to live under its own laws — Germans observing their own tribal customs and Romans continuing to be served by the Roman law. The only real difficulty to be solved was that of devising a system which might offer guidance in disputes between barbarians and Romans.

The Ostrogoths, Burgundians, Visigoths, and Vandals settled in the most advanced parts of the western Empire — in Italy, in the Rhone Valley, in southern Gaul and Spain, and in northern Africa. We know relatively little about the legal activities of the Vandal rulers, but the rulers of the other three nations left behind them impressive legal monuments to their efforts to provide good government for the territory which their people occupied. In all three cases, the Germanic followers of these barbarian kings constituted a minority of the population in their new kingdoms and the new rulers faced the problem of providing an administrative and legal system which would guarantee justice to both Germans and Roman provincials. This problem was handled in a slightly different way in each of the three kingdoms, but in all, the Germanic kings' activities reflect a real effort to behave in a manner acceptable at once to both Germanic and Roman parts of the population.

As we review the attempts of Ostrogothic, Burgundian, and Visigothic rulers to establish a system equitable to both parts of their population, it might be well to keep in mind that their efforts were not always appreciated by either Germans or Romans. Roman disaffection tended to be stronger than that of the Germans, for the Roman population found it difficult to respond to the overtures of its Germanic rulers who were heretics in religion — at the time of the establishment of their kingdoms, the rulers of all three of these barbarian nations (and their people) were Arian Christians. Nonetheless, these rulers behaved in an enlightened fashion

12

for the day. If situations over which they had no control had not developed, it is possible that their kingdoms might have been longer lasting than they were. But even though the Ostrogothic kingdom lasted for only a little less than fifty years, the Burgundian for something less than a hundred years, and the Visigothic for a little more than two hundred years, the legal activities of their Germanic kings rescued Roman law from possible oblivion and made possible its preservation in a form intelligible to the unsophisticated society of that day. Let us trace in some detail the "legislative" activities of Ostrogothic, Burgundian, and Visigothic kings.

The oldest surviving barbarian laws are fragments of a code issued by the Visigothic king Euric (466–485) about 481. Visigothic tradition indicated an earlier issuance of laws by Visigothic kings before the middle of the fifth century, but if these earlier laws ever were issued, they have not survived. Euric's code was issued for the use of the Visigoths in their suits with each other and probably for cases which arose between Goths and Romans — it reflects strong Roman influence, especially in use of written documents, in recognition of the last will or testament, and in provision for credit and interest transactions. In addition, Christian influence is reflected in regulations about marriage, especially impediments to marriage between those within the prohibited bonds of relationship.[1]

For the use of their Roman subjects, the early Visigothic kings sponsored the issuance of a special collection of Roman law considerably less complex than the *Theodosian Code* issued by the eastern Roman emperor Theodosius II in 438. The Visigothic code for Roman provincials was issued by Alaric II about 506 — it is known as the *Breviary of Alaric* or the *Lex Romana Visigothorum*. So far as Visigothic Spain was concerned, the *Breviary* remained in use among the Roman provincials only until the middle of the

[1] *Leges Visigothorum*, ed. Karl Zeumer, *Monumenta Germaniae Historica*, Legum Sectio I, Legum Nationum Germanicarum Tomus I (Hanover and Leipzig, 1902). A. K. Ziegler, *Church and State in Visigothic Spain* (Washington, D.C., 1930), p. 58.

WINGATE COLLEGE LIBRARY
WINGATE, N. C.

seventh century when a new collection of Visigothic law issued by King Recceswinth (in 654) offered a unified code for both Visigoths and Romans and prohibited the use of any code except this combined one. Thereafter the *Breviary* was prohibited in Visigothic Spain, but the influence of the *Breviary* did not come to an end. It remained in use among the inhabitants of southwestern Gaul and the Rhone Valley, both of which areas had come under Frankish rule in the early sixth century.[2]

The revised Visigothic code, issued in the mid-seventh century and corrected and expanded thereafter, is commonly known as the *Leges Visigothorum* or the *Forum Judicum*. It is from the second of these titles that the Spanish title, *Fuero Juzgo*, comes. The *Fuero Juzgo* is a thirteenth-century Castilian translation of the code incorporated in the *Siete Partidas* of Alfonso the Wise. Through the *Siete Partidas* Visigothic law was eventually to find its way to Spanish America and was even to influence the land law of the state of Texas.

To give us some indication of the tone of the Visigothic legislation, I quote here from the first title to Book II of the revised code as issued by King Erwig in 681:

Since there are those who base their cases on the amended laws, we declare in the first place and by way of introduction that just as the clarity of the laws is useful in settling controversies among the people, so too the obscurity of its provisions disturbs the order of justice. For often when good regulations are obscurely worded they provoke contradictions since they do not clearly prevent disputes between litigants and, while they ought to put an end to deceit, they produce new deceptive snares contrary to their own intention. Hence a variety of cases arise, hence are born the quarrels of the litigants and hence is born the uncertainty of the judges, so that they do not know how to reach a conclusion by ending or curbing deceit, which is assuredly always furthered by doubt and uncertainty. Therefore, since all matters which come into controversy cannot be confined in brief compass because of their confusion, at least those matters which have forced themselves on our royal attention by being discussed in public assemblies are, we decree, to be especially corrected in this book and are to be set in

[2] *Leges Visigothorum*, II, 1, 5, and II, 1, 10.

order with a clear and honest meaning, namely, expressing clear precepts for the doubtful, excellent ones for the injurious, more merciful for the condemned, broader for the narrow and completion for those only begun, whereby the peoples of our kingdom, whom the sole and manifest peace of our rule embraces, may thereafter be bound together and held fast by this establishment of corrected laws. Accordingly, let the correction of these laws and the orderly arrangement of our new sanctions, as it is set down in this book and in its ordered titles and as it is set forth in a subsequent compilation, assume validity, confirmed by our glory, upon all persons and peoples subject to the sovereignty of our highness, from the twelfth day before the Kalends of November of the second year of our reign, and let it be further validated by this unbreakable ordinance of our fame. We decree, moreover, that the laws which our glory promulgated against the excesses of the Jews are to be valid from the time when we confirmed them.[3]

We have in this constitution an example of the concern of the Visigothic legislators to improve their laws and to adjust them to the changing needs of their people, all distinction between Visigoth and Roman having disappeared with the conversion of the Visigoths to the Catholic form of Christianity, with the legalization of marriages between Goth and Roman, and with the simple passage of time. We also find in the quoted constitution an example of the excess verbosity of the Visigothic laws, a verbosity not normally found in the *leges barbarorum*. We find also an indication of the Visigothic attitude toward the Jewish population of the kingdom — amalgamation with this group was not encouraged and the Jews would continue to suffer under disabilities in Spain until the Moorish conquest in the early eighth century.

Before we leave the Visigoths, it might be well to point out that although the Visigoths accepted the personality of law principle during the early days of their kingdom and allowed the Roman population to retain its own system of law, this attitude gradually changed. By the mid-seventh century, Visigothic law had become

[3] Adapted from Ralph W. Ewton, Jr., "The Visigothic Code (Book II on Justice)," unpublished Master's Thesis in Rice University Library (Houston, Texas, 1961), pp. 68–69 (Book II, I, 1).

a territorial law, binding alike on all the inhabitants of the Visigothic kingdom.

The Burgundian nation seems to have been much smaller than
the Visigothic and its attempts to settle within the Roman Empire
suffered a number of setbacks. The first Burgundian kingdom, established in the area of the middle Rhine around Worms, lasted
only about twenty years before it fell to the invading Huns. Defeat by the Huns seems to have inflicted a fairly heavy loss of population on the Burgundians and it was only the remnants of the
tribe which a few years later received land farther to the south.
Here in the region of the upper Rhone Valley the Burgundians established a second kingdom on the understanding that they would
remain military allies of the Empire.

The Rhone Valley was one of the most advanced portions of the
western Empire. Its cities of Lyons and Vienne were centers of
late Roman education and culture. The arrival of the Burgundians
placed a barbarian people — uncouth and unlearned — in contact
with a sophisticated and highly literate Roman population.

The Burgundian people were settled on the soil by a system of
hospitality whereby the arable land was divided between a Roman
host and a barbarian guest. The Roman population had been declining for some time and the Burgundians were not numerous, so
this division does not seem to have caused any great economic dislocation in the region.

The reluctant willingness of the provincial Roman population
to receive Burgundian rule may well reflect the efforts on the part
of the Burgundian administration to adapt its customs to the new
conditions of settlement and to continue the old Roman political
and judicial arrangements. As in the case of the Visigoths, this effort necessitated a reduction to writing of the ancient Burgundian
law and a modification of that law to adjust it to the more settled
circumstances of Burgundian life. At the same time, the Burgundian rulers attempted to guarantee that the Roman part of the
population would continue to enjoy its rights and its own law. Accordingly, in the closing years of the fifth century and the early

years of the sixth century, the Burgundian king Gundobad and his son Sigismund issued codes for both the Burgundian and Roman parts of their population. The Germanic portion was issued in several sections between the years 483 and 532 and is known as the *Lex Burgundionum* or the *Lex Gundobada.* The laws for the Roman population were probably issued about the year 500 and collectively are known as the *Lex Romana Burgundionum.*[4]

These two law books had markedly different fates. The Burgundian kingdom was conquered by the Franks in 534, but this conquest did not mean the end of Burgundian law. The Franks, more than the other barbarians who entered the Empire, retained their respect for the personal conception of law and accordingly Frankish subjects of Burgundian descent continued to claim the right to be judged by Burgundian law for several centuries after the conquest. So Burgundian customary law as modified by contact with Roman provincials in the fifth century remained alive for many years and eventually contributed significantly to the development of a distinctive form of medieval law in southern France. On the other hand, the survival of the *Lex Romana Burgundionum* was very brief. When the Franks conquered the Burgundian kingdom, the *Lex Romana Burgundionum* was set aside and replaced by the *Breviary* of the Visigothic king Alaric. This development was not a disadvantage to the Roman population of the Rhone Valley, however, since the *Breviary* was a more complete statement of the Roman law than the *Lex Romana Burgundionum* had been. The *Breviary*, in an increasingly diluted form, would continue to have a shadowy existence in southern France until the revival of Roman law in the eleventh and twelfth centuries.

The Burgundian code is an extremely interesting collection of laws. Prominent among these laws are typical Germanic regulations about physical injuries. A tariff of payments is estabished covering a wide variety of physical blows and injuries, the penalty

---

[4] *Leges Burgundionum,* ed. L. R. deSalis, *Monumenta Germaniae Historica,* Legum Sectio I, Tomi II, Pars I (Hanover, 1892). *Gesetze der Burgunden,* ed. and tr. Franz Beyerle, *Germanenrechte,* X (Weimar, 1936).

for which was the payment of a money compensation to the injured party and a fine to the crown. For example, we find such provisions as these:

Whoever strikes a freeman shall pay a single solidus for each blow and in addition he shall pay a fine of six solidi to the king's treasury.[5]

Whoever strikes another's freeman shall pay a single semissis for each blow and the fine shall be four solidi.[6]

Whoever strikes another's slave shall pay a single tremissis for each blow and the fine shall be three solidi.[7]

In addition to such regulations establishing money payments in compensation for physical injuries, the Burgundian laws also recognized another typical Germanic institution, the wergeld. The various classes of Burgundian society were distinguished by their differing wergelds — the wergeld being the sum at which a man was valued and by the payment of which his death could be compensated. The laws reveal that the wergeld of the upper class of freemen was 300 solidi, that of the second class was 200 solidi, and that of the lowest class of freemen was 150 solidi.

At the same time that the Burgundian laws evidence the continued acceptance of such traditional customs as the money compensations and wergelds, they also reveal considerable outside influence. One of the clearest instances of this influence comes in connection with the inheritance laws. According to Germanic custom, the family lands were inalienable and passed to a man's descendants in accordance with fixed rules of succession. But this arrangement affected only those properties which were recognized as the common possession of the family — under Roman influence, property secured by other means than inheritance could be bought and sold or disposed of by written testament.[8] Other Roman influence is found in the composition of the Burgundian court which

---

[5] *Leges Burgundionum*, V, 1.

[6] *Leges Burgundionum*, V, 2.

[7] *Leges Burgundionum*, V, 3.

[8] K. F. Drew, "The Germanic Family of the *Leges Burgundionum*," *Medievalia et Humanistica*, Fascicle XVI (1963).

was presided over by two magistrates — a Roman and a Burgundian count.

Before leaving the Burgundian legal materials and passing to the Ostrogothic, we might attempt to isolate the attitude of the Burgundian lawgiver toward his work. To a certain extent Gundobad — like the other barbarian lawgivers — regarded his work as a recording of the customs of his people issued with the consent of the people. The conclusion of the Preface to the *Lex Burgundionum* states ". . . it is pleasing that our constitutions be confirmed with the signatures of the counts added below, so that this statement of the law which has been written as the result of our effort and *with the common consent of all* may, observed throughout posterity, maintain the validity of a lasting agreement." [9]

Although the Burgundian lawgiver was primarily concerned with the ancient customs of his people, he occasionally spoke in his capacity as supreme judge. In the example which follows Gundobad clearly stated the details of an unusual case which had been appealed to him. A decision had been rendered and was recorded in the code to serve as precedent for the future:

Since the facts of a criminal case which is pending between Fredegisil, our sword-bearer on the one side, and Balthamodus together with Aunegild on the other, have been heard and considered, we give an opinion which punishes this recent crime and imposes a method of restraint for the future.

Since Aunegild, after the death of her first husband, retaining her own legal competence, promised herself, not only with the consent of her relatives, but also with her own desire and will, to the above mentioned Fredegisil, and since she had received the greater part of the wedding price which her betrothed had paid, she broke her pledged faith, having been aroused by the ardor of her desire for Balthamodus. Furthermore, she not only violated her vows, but repeated her customary shameful union, and on account of this, she ought to atone for such a crime and such a violation of her free status not otherwise than with the pouring forth of her own blood. Nevertheless we command, placing reverence for these holy days before public punishment, that Aunegild, deprived of

[9] *Leges Burgundionum*, Preface.

honor by human and divine judgment, should pay her wergeld, that is three hundred solidi, to Fredegisil under compulsion.

Nor do we remove merited condemnation from Balthamodus who presumed to receive a woman due in marriage to another man, for his case deserves death. But in consideration of the holy days, we recall our sentence for his execution, under the condition that he should be compelled to pay his wergeld of one hundred fifty solidi to that Fredegisil unless he can offer public oath with eleven oathhelpers in which he affirms that at that time in which he was united with the abovementioned Aunegild as if by the right of marriage, he was unaware that she was pledged to Fredegisil. If he shall so swear, let him suffer neither loss nor punishment.

In truth we command that the judgment set forth in this case be established to remain the law forever, and lest the moderation of the composition now permitted encourage anyone hereafter to commit a deed of such great crime, we command that whosoever incurs the guilt of such a deed not only may sustain the loss of his property, but also may be punished by the loss of his life. For it is preferable that the multitude be corrected by the condemnation of a few rather than that the appearance of unsuitable moderation introduce a pretext which may contribute to the license of delinquency.[10]

Here there is little doubt that the Burgundian king was no longer acting as a law compiler or even as a lawgiver — he was acting as a judge and lawmaker.

The Ostrogoths appeared in northern Italy at the close of the fifth century and, with the approval of the east Roman emperor, established a kingdom nominally dependent on Constantinople. The land of Italy was shared between Ostrogoths and Romans, but as in the case of the Burgundians, this division of land does not seem to have worked much hardship on the Roman population, for the Italian peninsula had been suffering for some time from depopulation.

Ostrogothic rule in Italy did not bring a radical break with the past. The Ostrogoths had had military and commercial contacts with the eastern Empire for a long period before their migration into Italy. In addition, their king Theodoric had been brought up

[10] *Leges Burgundionum,* LII, 2–5.

in Constantinople as a hostage of the Empire and there he had acquired a great respect for Roman civilization and administration. Consequently, the administration of the Ostrogothic kingdom was a conscious adoption of the former Roman administration: even in the matter of personnel, the administration remained much the same, for Theodoric made extensive use of Romans in official positions — Boethius and Cassiodorus being simply the best known of the Roman officials whom he employed.

Theodoric attempted to narrow the breach between the Gothic and Roman elements in his kingdom's population. He was not entirely successful — the Romans resented the Arianism of the Goths and the Goths resented the deliberate policy of Romanization urged by Theodoric. Nonetheless as long as Theodoric lived, the attempt at amalgamation was a reasonably successful one. Had Theodoric been succeeded by a ruler as able as himself and had the Byzantine Empire not seen fit to intervene in Italy, it is possible that the Ostrogoths would have been at least as successful as the Visigoths in fusing the two racial elements. Such speculation is idle, of course, since the Ostrogoths had little chance to prove the success of Theodoric's policy of Romanization because of their conquest by Byzantium in the mid-sixth century.

In the field of law, the Ostrogoths retained their customary law (still unwritten) in disputes among themselves, whereas the Romans continued to be governed according to Roman law. In contrast with the Visigothic and Burgundian kingdoms where disputes between German and Roman were to be settled according to the Germanic law, in Ostrogothic Italy disputes between Goth and Roman were to be settled according to Roman law. Inasmuch as the *Theodosian Code* was not a very satisfactory code of law since it contained only the imperial edicts of the emperors from Constantine I to Theodosius II, a new and more inclusive, albeit simpler, statement of law was needed. For this purpose Theodoric issued an abbreviated code known as the *Edict of Theodoric*.[11] This *Edict* remained in force in Italy until the arrival of the Lom-

---

[11] *Edictum Theodorici*, ed. F. Bluhme, *Monumenta Germaniae Historica*, Leges Sectio I, Tomus V (Hanover, 1875–1879).

bards even though the classic collection of Roman law, the *Corpus Iuris Civilis*, was promulgated in Italy following the Byzantine conquest. But Byzantine rule was never completely established in Italy during the brief period between the downfall of the Ostrogothic Kingdom in 551 and the arrival of the Lombards in 568. Consequently, the influence of the *Corpus Iuris Civilis* was to be limited to those relatively small areas along the northeastern coast around Ravenna and at the tip of the Italian peninsula which remained under Byzantine control for several centuries.

A survey of the legislation and judicial activities of the Lombard kings will conclude this study. But before we turn to the Lombards, it might be well to note very briefly the work of several other early Germanic kings who ruled kingdoms established in territory which had once been part of the Roman Empire. Here, either Roman administration had been weakening for some time, as in the case of Britain, or the territory was so far from the center of Roman culture, as in northern Gaul, that the presence of a sizable Roman population did not present quite the same problem as faced the Germanic kingdoms in Spain, southern Gaul, or Italy.

Neither the Frankish kings nor the Anglo-Saxon kings undertook a collection of Roman law. In the case of Britain, it seems that the break with the Roman past was sufficiently complete that the survival of a large Roman population was not a problem to be reckoned with. Accordingly, the Anglo-Saxon dooms show very little influence of Roman law (if we except the influence obviously exercised by the Church). The Anglo-Saxon dooms — written in the vernacular and not in Latin as were all the other early codes — provide us with information about Germanic customs which had been little if at all affected by contact with Rome.[12]

The Frankish laws are very controversial. It is usually assumed that the collection of Salian laws was issued toward the close of the fifth century and that the collection of Ripuarian laws was issued about a hundred years later. These laws reflect little Roman

---

[12] F. Liebermann, *Die Gesetze der Angelsachsen* (Halle, 1903–1916); F. L. Attenborough, *The Laws of the Earliest English Kings* (Cambridge, 1922); and A. J. Robertson, *The Laws of the Kings of England from Edmund to Henry I* (Cambridge, 1925).

influence nor do they reflect any Christian influence. If their date
and contents were not so suspect, the Frankish laws would provide
us with one of our best sources for pure Germanic custom.[13]

It is not clear what the Franks did about the Roman population
of the territory which they conquered. Inasmuch as they allowed
the *Breviary* to remain in use in southern Gaul after their conquest of that territory from the Visigoths and Burgundians, one
assumes that they were not hostile to Roman law. Furthermore,
the Frankish insistence on the personality-of-law principle would
have encouraged the retention of Roman law by the Roman
part of the population. The Ripuarian law specifically provides:
"Whenever anyone in the district of Ripuaria is called into court
— whether he be Frank, Burgundian, or Alamannian — let him
answer according to the law of his nation." [14] No mention is made
here of the Romans, however, and the later absence of a famili-
arity with Roman law in northern Gaul encourages the conclusion
that the settlement of suits according to Roman law received little,
if any, encouragement from the Franks.

The Lombards were the last major Germanic people to invade
the Empire. They entered in the second half of the sixth century,
invading an Italy torn by a long-drawn-out war between Ostrogothic Kingdom and the Byzantine Empire. The Byzantines had
at last won the war and established a provincial administration in
Italy, but before Byzantine rule could become well established,
the Lombards invaded from the north and with relatively little
difficulty overcame the weak Byzantine garrisons which had been
left in the major towns. The Italo-Roman population seems to
have stood passively aside and to have observed the successful
entry of the Lombards — perhaps Lombard rule promised relief
from the heavy Byzantine taxation.

[13] *Capitularia Regum Francorum*, ed. A. Boretius, *Monumenta Germaniae Historica*, Legum Sectio II, Tomus I (Hanover, 1883) . *Lex Ribuaria*, ed. Franz Beyerle and Rudolf Buchner, *Monumenta Germaniae Historica*, Legum Sectio I, Legum Nationum Germanicarum, Tomi III, Pars II (Hanover, 1954) .

[14] Adapted from James Pierce Barefield, "The Ripuarian Code: A Translation
with Introduction," unpublished Master's Thesis in Rice University Library (Houston, Texas, 1958) , XXXV, 3 (p. 34) .

An objective history of Lombard Italy is difficult to write since the Lombards were opposed by a very vocal enemy which lost no opportunity to point out the barbarity and cruelty of the Lombards and their lack of any redeeming features. The Arian heresy of the Lombards was responsible for the initial friction between papacy and barbarians, but after the conversion of the Lombards to the Catholic form of Christianity in the seventh century, papal hostility was occasioned more by fear of incorporation in the Lombard state than by any national vices characteristic of the Lombard people.

If, however, we ignore the statements made by papal and Frankish chroniclers and consider only the written materials left by the Lombards themselves, a picture emerges which is not radically different from the experience of the Visigoths and Burgundians in their attempts to rule a more culturally advanced people than themselves and to provide an administration which could protect the lives and property of both Germanic and Roman subjects.

Although the Lombard judges were learned only in the Lombard law and the Lombard courts do not seem to have offered a means of settling disputes among the Roman part of the population, it is clear from the Lombard legislation that the Lombards recognized Roman law as continuing to live in Italy and that the Roman part of their population continued to settle their disputes and to regulate their legal transactions in accordance with it. It is not clear how this Roman law was administered, for unlike the situation in the Ostrogothic, Visigothic, and Burgundian kingdoms, the Lombard courts took no cognizance of Roman law. Yet we have clear indications that a form of Roman law survived. Title 153 of Liutprand's laws provides that if a Lombard man entered the church, the children who were born before his consecration "shall live by that law as he lived when he begot them." Presumably clerics became subject to the Roman law of the Church and the law just cited prevented the children of clerics from claiming also to be subject to its jurisdiction. Another of Liutprand's laws states that those who draw up charters shall draw them up either

24

"according to the law of the Lombards or according to that of the Romans." So even if the Lombard kings issued no collection of Roman laws for their Roman subjects and provided no tribunals learned in the Roman law, it is nonetheless clear that the Lombard kings recognized the survival of Roman law and legal forms.

The value of the Lombard legislation lies in the continuing legislative activity of the Lombard kings and the development of legal reasoning revealed in the successive issues of these laws. The earliest laws issued by the Lombards were issued by Rothair in 643 in a law code known as *Rothair's Edict*. The term "legislation" can hardly be applied to this code, for *Rothair's Edict* is almost entirely Germanic custom modified only slightly by the experiences encountered by the Lombards in the process of migrating into and settling in Italy. A brief supplement to *Rothair's Edict* was added by Grimwald in 668, and a long series of supplements (153 laws) was issued by King Liutprand between 713 and 735. Finally, brief additions were made by Ratchis in 745 and 746 and by Aistulf in 750 and 755.[15]

We might trace very briefly the increasingly sophisticated legal reasoning of the Lombard lawgivers.

Rothair's Edict is, as noted above, usually regarded as a statement of almost pure Germanic custom. I quote here briefly from a long tariff of compositions to be paid in cases of very diverse physical injury:

In the matter of composition for blows and injuries which are inflicted by one freeman on another freeman, composition is to be paid according to the procedure provided below, the blood-feud being outlawed.[16]

He who strikes another on the head so that the skin which the hair covers is broken, shall pay 6 solidi as composition. He who strikes two blows, shall pay 12 solidi as composition. If there are three blows, he shall pay 18 solidi. If there are more blows than this num-

[15] *Leges Langobardorum*, ed. F. Bluhme, *Monumenta Germaniae Historica*, Legum Tomus IIII (Hanover, 1868). Franz Beyerle, *Die Gesetze der Langobarden* (Weimar, 1947).
[16] *Leges Langobardorum*, Rothair 45.

ber, they are not to be counted but composition shall be paid for three only.[17]

He who strikes another on the head so that the bones are broken, shall pay 12 solidi as composition if one bone is broken. He shall pay 24 solidi as composition if two bones are broken; 36 solidi for three. If there were more broken than this, they are not to be counted . . .[18]

If anyone strikes out another's eye, he shall pay half the wergeld of the injured party as composition.[19]

He who cuts off another's nose shall pay half of that one's wergeld as composition.[20]

He who cuts off another's lip, shall pay 16 solidi as composition. And if one, two, or three teeth are thereby revealed, he shall pay 20 solidi as composition.[21]

The tariff continues in great detail, the payments varying according to the rank of the injured party.

Rothair's Edict also indicates that compurgation was the normal method of proof employed in determining the relative rights of a party to his suit. Compurgation was a mode of proof whereby one of the parties to a suit, usually the defendant, swore his innocence and his oath was supported by a number of oathtakers or oathhelpers (the precise number to be offered being determined by the court). If the oath of the defendant and his helpers was pure, the innocence of the party was presumably established. If, however, the oath was broken, then the guilt of the party was thereby established. *Rothair's Edict* defines a broken oath as follows: "An oath is known to be broken when he who is accused, joined by his oathtakers, does not dare to swear on the holy gospels or consecrated weapons, or if he or one of his oathtakers withdraws from the oath: then the oath is known to be broken." [22]

The laws issued by Liutprand a little less than a hundred years later are considerably more advanced than these of Rothair. There

---

[17] *Leges Langobardorum*, Rothair 46.
[18] *Leges Langobardorum*, Rothair 47.
[19] *Leges Langobardorum*, Rothair 48.
[20] *Leges Langobardorum*, Rothair 49.
[21] *Leges Langobardorum*, Rothair 50.
[22] *Leges Langobardorum*, Rothair 363.

is even some indication of doubt that proof by combat or by torture would necessarily establish the truth. Here is a law from the year 724:

If anyone accuses another man of theft and overcomes him in combat, or if perhaps the theft is revealed through torture by a public official and composition has been made, and afterwards it is found that the theft was committed by another man and it appears to be certain that he who first paid the composition did not steal the property: then he who paid the composition shall receive back all those things which he paid from him to whom he paid them, and that one shall pay composition who afterwards was found to be the thief . . .[23]

From the same year (724) we have this law concerning the liability of a man's son for the father's debts:

If a man incurs a debt and sells his property and the debt is still such that he cannot repay it, and if his son has acquired anything through his wife or by his own efforts, after the father has sold all of his property or given it to his creditors for his debt or it has been confiscated by a public official, the creditor may not seek by force those properties which the son secured from his wife or through his own efforts. However, if the son is accused by his father's creditors of having commended something or hidden something from the property of his father or mother, he shall offer oath that he has commended or hidden nothing, and he shall be absolved. And if afterwards he is found to have any of the paternal property, he shall pay an eightfold composition.[24]

And one final law from the year 733:

It has been announced to us that a certain man has a well in his courtyard and, according to custom, there is a prop and lift for raising the water. Another man coming along stood under that lift and, when a certain man came to draw water from that well and incautiously released the lift, it came down on him who stood under it and he was killed. The question then arose concerning the problem of who should pay composition for the death of that one and it has been referred to us. It seems right to us and to our judges that that man who was killed, since he was not an animal but had the power of reason just as a man ought to have, should have

[23] *Leges Langobardorum*, Liutprand 56.
[24] *Leges Langobardorum*, Liutprand 57.

looked into what place he had set himself to stand or what weight was above himself. Therefore two parts of the price of his composition shall be reckoned to him [the dead man] and the third part of the amount at which he was valued according to the edict shall be paid in composition by that one who incautiously drew the water. And he shall give the composition to the children or the near relatives who are his heirs and the case shall be ended without any feud or grievance because it was done unintentionally. Moreover, that one whose well it is should have no blame because if we placed the blame on him, afterwards no one would permit others to raise water from their wells and because all men are not able to have a well, the rest who are poor would die and also those traveling through would suffer need.[25]

The Lombard laws seem to have had a longer lasting influence than any other of the *leges barbarorum* with the possible exception of the Visigothic. The Lombard kingdom fell in 774 to conquest by Charlemagne and the Franks, but the Italian portion of Charlemagne's empire remained organized as a separate territory and the Lombard laws remained in effect, supplemented from time to time by capitularies issued by Charlemagne and his Carolingian successors.

It is convenient to close the period of the barbarian kings with the fall of the Lombard kingdom in the late eighth century. By that time the Germanic and Roman elements of the population had essentially fused. With this racial fusion had come a legal fusion and in the new feudal law which developed in the ninth and tenth centuries, it is hard to determine which portions are Germanic in origin and which are Roman in origin. Pirenne may have been right in directing attention away from the fifth century as the end of the ancient world and the beginning of the Middle Ages, but instead of putting the break at the beginning of the eighth century with the Mohammedan conquest of the southern and western shores of the Mediterranean Sea, perhaps it should be put at the end of the eighth century with the cessation of the stream of barbarian legislation based on the assumption that the Germanic and

[25] *Leges Langobardorum*, Liutprand 136.

Roman elements of the population were distinct and each should have its own law. By the end of the eighth century the last distinct remnants of the Roman world had gone and a true medieval culture had been produced instead — a culture grossly vulgarized, if we compare it with that of ancient Rome, but a culture significantly advanced if we compare it with the rude culture of the original Germanic barbarians.

⟫ ROBERT S. LOPEZ ⟪

OF TOWNS AND TRADE

To A modern layman, the expression "of towns and trade" may seem redundant and almost tautological. We can hardly think of towns without trade, or of trade without towns. This is what Henri Pirenne had in mind when he explained the urban revival of the later Middle Ages by the striking formula *ville et marché*, town equals market. The equation holds for the latest thousand years, but it does not fit the earlier phases of urban history. To place ourselves in the historical context of the early Middle Ages, there is no better beginning than disentangling the two notions of towns and trade.[1]

[1] The multilingual symposium *La Città nell'alto Medioevo*, Settimane di Studio del Centro Italiano di Studi sull'Alto Medioevo VI (Spoleto, 1959), is the best and most recent general discussion of early medieval urban history. Its bibliographic references, and those of my paper, "The Crossroads within the Walls," in O. Handlin and J. Burchard, eds., *The Historian and the City* (Cambridge, Mass., 1963), will introduce the reader to more detailed study. In English, one may use H. van Werveke's Chapter 1 of the *Cambridge Economic History*, III (Cambridge, Eng., 1963; but the chapter was written in 1940), and, for trade, M. M. Postan's and R. S. Lopez's Chapters 4 and 5 of the *Cambridge Economic History*, II (Cambridge, Eng., 1952; but my chapter was written in 1946).

Among later works on the early medieval town (not listed in the Spoleto symposium), the following have been most helpful to me: *L'artisanat et la vie urbaine en Pologne médiévale*, Ergon III (Warsaw, 1962); J. Dhondt, "Les problèmes de Quentovic," in *Studi in Onore di Amintore Fanfani*, I (Milan, 1962); G. Fasoli, "Che cosa sappiamo delle città italiane nell'alto medio evo," *Vierteljahrschrift für*

Of Towns and Trade

When Gregory of Tours, the historian of Merovingian France, wanted to single out the factors that made a city, he stated: "I cannot understand why this center [he was speaking of Dijon] does not bear the title of city. Yet it has precious sources in its vicinity. Moreover, to the west side it has very fertile slopes, covered with vineyards from which the inhabitants draw a Falernum of such high class that they look down upon Chalon wine." Perhaps the people of Dijon should not have been so conceited: Chalon wine is one of Burgundy's best. What matters, however, is that Gregory was convinced that a town so well endowed with spirits ought to have its official consecration as a city, that is, get a bishop. The question of whether or not Dijon had any significant trade did not worry him in the least. And in this, he agreed with all of his contemporaries.

Gregory of Tours' notions substantially coincided with those of the very inventors of the word "city" (*civitas*), the Romans. In their eyes, the test of cityhood, if I may use this word, was the existence of a public square for political meetings and discussions, of a public bathhouse for the comfort of the body, and of a theater or arena for the pleasures of the mind. Such a threefold test could be met by any self-governing community of landowners and of civil, military, and religious officials, even if there were virtually no merchants or craftsmen in it. And even in the Roman urban centers where merchants were numerous and affluent, they enjoyed little status and usually played no leading role in the body politic and cultural life of the city.

It was the Arabs who first included in their "test of cityhood," instead of the public square, the bazaar or market. What they had in mind, however, was not so much the economic function of the market as the facility it offered for social intercourse. As a matter

Sozial- und Wirtschaftsgeschichte, XLVII (1960); G. Galasso, "Le città campane nell'alto Medioevo," *Archivio Storico per le Province Napoletane*, new ser., XXXVIII–XXXIX (1958–1959); L. de Valdeavellano, *Sobre los burgos y los burgueses de la Espana medieval* (Madrid, 1960); F. Vercauteren, "De la cité antique à la commune médiévale," *Bulletin de l'Académie Royale de Belgique*, Classe des Lettres, 5th ser., XLVIII (1962). This brief list does not aim at completeness.

of fact, public squares fitted neither their political needs nor their urbanistic tastes; their towns were not self-governing, and the clannish privacy of small and unshaded inner courts attracted them more than an indiscrete mixing in a common, sun-drenched open space. The Arabs also replaced the materialistic amusements of the arena with the uplifting entertainments of the cathedral mosque, that is, a mosque endowed with a Friday preacher. Thus, in the Islamic world of the early Middle Ages, only one of the three pillars of the Roman city remained unshaken: the public bathhouse.

Byzantine cities, besides keeping the bathhouse, clung longer to the arena and the public square, but eventually transferred the center of social activity to the church and the market. Town autonomy in the Byzantine Empire was not much greater than in the Islamic world; religion played an equally significant role. In Western Europe, however, the early medieval town preserved so little of its economic and political importance that neither the market nor the public square survived; as for bathhouses, the less said about them the better. This left the church alone to meet the test of cityhood as best it could; hence Gregory of Tours' insistence on the right of Dijon to uphold its status by obtaining an episcopal cathedral. Indeed, the open space before the cathedral or another important church was normally the sole meeting place, the center of social and economic activities in the early medieval West.

All this is well and good, one might say, but if ancient, early medieval, and late medieval cities were so thoroughly different, what is the purpose in comparing them? To this, the answer is that all cities in history, from Memphis, Egypt, to Memphis, Tennessee, have something in common. They all are, if I may repeat what I already suggested on another occasion, crossroads within a circle, meeting places of people who through both their diversity and their togetherness create an original, unique compound. A town is at once a keeper of tradition and an accelerator of change. It does not have to be large in order to be great, or, at least, significant; its size, its wealth, its power, all quantitative characteristics matter less than the quality of its inhabitants. What makes a town, says Isidore of Seville in the seventh century, is "not stones, but men." More than a thousand years earlier, a Greek poet, Alcaeus, had said much the same thing in a subtler way: "Not houses finely roofed or well built walls, not canals or dockyards make a city, but men able to use their opportunity."

Early medieval trade without towns is much harder to track down, for towns are to the history of illiterate and half-literate ages what bones are to paleontology, namely, the only enduring and recognizable traces one can find. Virtually every recorded event, when records are few, carries a reference to an urban site; and if all books are mute, one can dig and interpret stones. Trade, on the contrary, is not unmistakably engraved in the surviving materials. Even if we come across a datable ecclesiastic heirloom or a hoard of coins, usually we cannot tell for sure whether the objects were obtained from merchants, or looted, or given in lieu of salary, or received as a present. Moreover, early medieval writers do not enjoy talking about commerce and the bloodless, godless pursuit of riches any more than Victorian writers liked mentioning underwear, both being considered as coarse, albeit indispensable, matters.

Still, coarse matters will out, however much one tries to repress them. References to itinerant merchants, sometimes to the pedlars so dear to old-fashioned textbooks of medieval history, more often to respectable businessmen, or even to impressive ones, are conspicuous enough to assure us that much trade had no permanent roots in any particular town. No town is mentioned, for instance, as the fixed home of the Rhadanite Jews, who in the Carolingian period shuttled between Spain and China through inland Europe and central Asia. Again, trade was an occasional, part-time activity for many people who made a living chiefly through agricultural occupations in wholly rural surroundings. The Frisians and Scandinavians used both commerce and warfare as supplementary sources of income and temporary relaxation from cultivating their fields. Abbeys in France and manors in England had agents, *negotiatores*, or stewards, who were first and foremost administrators

33

of real estate, but also carried out some business, in behalf of both their employers and themselves. Even the doge of Venice, in the ninth century, while attending to affairs of state and real estate, found time to engage in commercial ventures at sea.

One might object that Venice was a city. In the early Middle Ages, it was and it was not. Its very name — a plural, in Latin — indicates that the first Venice was a community of fishermen and salt makers scattered on the innumerable islets of the lagoon. The main center of the community wandered from Heraclea to Malamocco, from Malamocco to Rialto, where it eventually settled after winking at other possible sites such as Torcello, Murano, Caorle. In northern Europe, the seminomadic character of commercial meeting places was often so pronounced that they left no identifiable traces above ground. Indeed, there is a raging controversy as to which of the meager remains found underground here and there near the mouth of the Canche River marks the spot of Quentovic, for two or three centuries the main disembarking place on the Continent for English men and wares. Duurstede, at some time the political and economic capital of the Frisians, sprang up from nothing and vanished into nothingness. Long before the Danes built the first permanent settlement of Visby, the late medieval urban center in Gotland Island, Gotland was a crossroads of trade; but no buildings belonging to the early Middle Ages have left any trace on or beneath its ground.

It is not enough, however, to acknowledge the existence of early medieval towns and trade (whether separately or jointly); we also would like to obtain some information about the size of both towns and trade. Unfortunately, the extant sources will not supply any precise answer. They will not enable us to pass final judgment on the *cause célèbre* that has generated so much heat since it was opened by Alfons Dopsch and Henri Pirenne: whether the low point of Western European life was reached in the Merovingian or the Carolingian period. It certainly was a fruitful, stimulating controversy while it lasted, but we have now reached the point of diminishing returns. Perhaps I may sum up the present deadlock with the same words which I used a number of years ago, at the International Congress of Rome, without shocking any of the learned listeners: "The earlier centuries of the early Middle Ages benefited from the fact that Roman roads and towns, institutions and traditions, had not entirely disintegrated, and that disheartened Roman personnel still lent a hand to inexperienced barbarians. The later centuries benefited from the fact that the further shrinking of the legacy of antiquity forced the new world to make its first clumsy attempts at reorganizing roads, towns, institutions, and traditions with a personnel of mixed blood and rudimentary training. Whether this pale dawn was better or worse than the previous pale dusk is anybody's guess . . . exact economic comparisons between two adjoining and similar periods cannot be made without some statistical base."

Only when the tenth century sets in do we see indubitable signs of growth; to this growth I shall devote the concluding remarks of an inevitably short survey. But for the earlier period, the half-millennium that is most commonly called "Dark Ages," the utmost I can do is to outline quantitative boundaries that no reasonable guesser ought to overstep through excessive optimism or excessive pessimism, then to describe tentatively as many types of towns and aspects of trade as the scant evidence warrants.

We should not pay too much attention to the adjectives "large," "populous," or "opulent" that a chronicler or a charter may bestow upon a town: usually, such complimentary expressions are no better indications of size than the words "His Highness" as applied to a prince, or "great man" as applied to a football coach. But it is sometimes possible for us to map and measure the walled area of an early medieval town. If we can also find some written or archaeological information concerning the thickness of settlement within the walls and the possible existence of suburbs, we are on good ground to assess tentatively the physical stature of that center and to suggest the most likely size of other centers in the same class.

Gdansk (Danzig), whose walled area in the tenth century encompassed barely seven acres, may probably be regarded as a typical example of the lowest step in the early medieval urban ladder.

It would be hard to believe that seven acres sufficed for the development of an urban microcosm, if we did not know from archaeological evidence that, apart from a few seigneurial buildings, Gdansk was a compact cluster of tiny houses, or rather shacks, whose inhabitants lived in what would seem today intolerable crowding. Yet it had a number of craftsmen, carried out some long-distance trade, and played a role in the administration of the country. Tenth-century Poland was a newcomer to "civilization" (if civilization means town life, as it did to the Romans), and its urbanism could not but be crude.

Older countries boasted of somewhat larger cities. Paris, within the limits of the Île de la Cité, covered slightly more than twenty acres, and by the tenth century was already expanding into diminutive suburbs on both the northern and the southern bank of the Seine. Again, this may seem very little for the capital of Hugh Capet; but Hugh Capet maintained only a handful of retainers, the archiepiscopal see remained at Sens, the fair of near-by St. Denis attracted merchants only for a short season, and the teachers of theology and medicine had not yet moved to the Latin Quarter from Rheims, Laon, and other centers of northern France. One might even contend that ninth-century Paris was less large than another island city in faraway Sweden, Birka, at that time the turnstile of commercial exchanges linking Russia to England. The walled area of Birka enclosed a surface almost double that of Paris: thirty-five acres. Archaeology, however, indicates that a good proportion of the inner space never had any permanent buildings.

The strongest urban traditions and the largest towns in Catholic Europe were in Italy, close to the Byzantine and Muslim world. Milan's walled area, in the ninth century, still measured two hundred eighty acres, as it did when a Roman emperor resided there. It is true that in the very center of the city there was a small wood, where the archbishop went hunting; but the remaining surface was thickly settled, and suburban buildings were sprouting along the eleven roads or trails that converged toward the gates. The walls of Rome enclosed an area twelve times as large as that of Milan, and so did those of Constantinople; but

Constantinople belonged to another world, and Rome consisted of scattered live sections in the midst of a ghost town. Hence Milan may be regarded as the largest urban center in early medieval Catholic Europe.

It would be interesting, but hazardous, to translate surfaces into population figures. Should we adopt a flat basis of fifty inhabitants per acre, which might seem too generous to most historians, we would obtain figures ranging from 350 people for Gdansk to 14,000 for Milan. Fourteen thousand inhabitants are an unimpressive group, not only by modern standards, but also by late medieval counts: by the end of the thirteenth century, both Milan and Venice must have been close to 200,000 inhabitants, and Florence, Genoa, and Paris to 100,000. This makes it only more remarkable that the 350 people (or fewer) gathered in Gdansk were enough to plant a seed of urban life in one of the most underdeveloped parts of Europe.

Vague though these evaluations may seem, they are closer approximations than any we can hope for concerning the volume of trade. What figures we occasionally come across in the written sources refer to individual transactions, mostly carried out in behalf of exceptional customers such as princes or prelates, or in privileged surroundings such as the outer regions near the Byzantine or Islamic borders. No doubt it is interesting that in the eighth century a Lombard abbess and daughter of a king disbursed 5,488 gold solidi in cash to buy real estate, and still more interesting that in 829 a Venetian doge invested 1,200 librae of silver deniers in maritime trade, but neither figure is a clue to the over-all size of commerce.

Numismatic evidence is more helpful, but cannot provide the sweeping answers some historians have asked of it. No matter how many coins we find in a hoard, we cannot tell what proportion of the total circulation they represent, or how much trade was carried out by payments in kind. The latter should not be dismissed as mere barter: normally the mediums used were essential chattels or commodities such as horses, oxen, or grain, whose value in cash was specifically mentioned or traditionally known. Bread loaves or squares of cloth of a standard size were sometimes used as fractional currency. In twelfth-century Russia, pelts of squirrel with the seal of the prince played almost the role of paper money. Still, hard coins have special significance, and a study of the prevalent types suggests the following tentative conclusions.

First of all, there never was a complete absence of coinage. Throughout Catholic Europe, new coins were struck by the thousands, some of them in royal mints, others by lower governmental officials, others by private, independent manufacturers. Foreign currency or ancient coins were available to supplement the domestic production. All this indicates continuity in commerce. Granted that coins are also used to store wealth, measure the value of other goods, pay taxes and fines, and adorn necklaces and bracelets, there would have been no incentive to strike or import them if they could never be used for buying or selling.

Second, the production and circulation of coins dwindled more and more. Even though the number of extant coins is not a precise indication of the number of coins that actually existed at a given time, the extreme rarity or total lack of coins that can be ascribed to certain periods of the early Middle Ages can hardly be a mere accident. Moreover, the largest monetary unit of the ancient world, the gold solidus, ceased to be struck; its fractions and, later, silver coins were used in its place. Inasmuch as the cost of striking three tremisses (thirds of a solidus) was exactly three times the cost of striking one solidus, the fact that the latter was discontinued indicates that the tremisses were the largest units the traffic would bear. The shift from gold coinage to silver coinage may be ascribed to political considerations which need not be recalled here; but the fact that Charlemagne endeavored vainly to increase the weight of his silver denier, and that the denier precipitously dwindled in silver content, seems to confirm nonmonetary evidence that the over-all volume of trade diminished greatly.

Third, what coins were struck were still endowed with a comparatively strong purchasing power (a power further increased by the fall of prices in the early Middle Ages), whereas small silver and copper coins, the instruments of retail trade and everyday purchases, entirely vanished. This suggests the conclusion that luxury trade and large-scale buying and selling survived better than daily exchanges. A merchant or a prince could fill his purse with enough money to purchase the most expensive things, but an ordinary citizen could not find the small change he might need to buy a drink or a trinket in the nearest shop.

The problem, however, is whether shops survived at all. This brings us back to the other half of our topic, towns: What did they look like? What did they live on? What were the principal urban types?

Inevitably, one thinks first of the distinction between towns of new foundation and towns of Roman origin, a distinction, to be sure, that exists only in that part of Europe which had been under Roman rule. Some of the latter, though probably not the majority, continued to live and play an urban role throughout the early Middle Ages; the pattern of survival, however, was not uniform. Milan, for some time one of the capitals of the later Roman Empire, suffered all kinds of military disasters and administrative setbacks without ever losing its paramount economic and intellectual position among northern Italian cities; Ravenna, which succeeded Milan as a Roman capital, remained the capital of the Byzantine possessions in Italy, but by the tenth century was eclipsed by upstart Venice and settled down in urban mediocrity. Tournai, one of the several supply centers of the Roman army on the northern frontier, was chosen by the Merovingian kings as their first capital, thus escaping the gradual extinction of nearly all towns in what is Belgium today; it maintained a fairly important position throughout the Middle Ages and the early modern period, but never made the grade as one of the dominant cities of the region. Aosta, whose Roman and early medieval urban past still speaks from its gridiron pattern, ancient theater and arch, and medieval churches and walls, had perhaps the most striking consistency of development: it was the natural center of a valley enclosed by the Alps, which both protected and hemmed in its modest but indispensable urban functions. Lyons, once the capital of Roman Gaul, also never stopped exploiting its central position at the confluence of two great rivers; but it grew with France, and hence changed its physical shape. Even its oldest section has become a maze of meandering alleys, where no Roman memory is visible above the ground. This reminds us that probably the worst enemies of ancient buildings and street plans are not the barbarians, but the town developers.

The cities just mentioned can be followed through the "Dark Ages" and down to our own days, thanks to an almost unbroken series of written and archaeological records. Series of this kind are seldom available. When the record is discontinuous, can we still postulate continuity of urban life wherever a modern town occupies the site and bears the name of a Roman one? This would lead us to include in the count all the important cities of northern Italy but three: Venice, Ferrara, and Alessandria. And even in England, where most modern cities have no ancient pedigree, it has been observed that all but one of the pre-urban nodes that emerged in the ninth century as minting centers were located in places previously known as Roman towns.

Nevertheless, it would be unwise to assume automatically a continual development, since the only link to the Roman past may have been a comparatively undamaged public building, or merely its recoverable stones, or nothing but the attraction of a favorable geographic location. Most English historians believe that Roman Londinium was completely deserted after the Anglo-Saxons conquered it; but the road crossing the Thames could not be obliterated, the fallen stones were handy; by the seventh century there was a new agglomeration which became the capital of Essex and from that time continued to grow. Budapest — to mention another modern capital — is partly built on the site of Roman Aquincum, whose amphitheater was used by the Lombards in the sixth century and by the Magyars ever since the tenth; but in the intermediate period, under the Avars, the settlement entirely vanished. The principal town of modern Dalmatia, Spalato or Split, was the by-product not of a Roman town but of Emperor Diocletian's country mansion: its medieval walls are the external wall of

Diocletian's palace, its main square the central hall, its cathedral the former imperial mausoleum.

One would think that a favorable geographic location — a ford, a natural harbor, a gap between mountain chains, a hill overlooking a fertile plain — can never lose its appeal. This is often true, even in those parts of Europe never under Roman rule. Lübeck, a small Slav settlement before becoming a German city, was twice destroyed and rebuilt in the twelfth century. Its location on the estuary of the Trave River and at the neck of the Danish-Holstein peninsula separating the North Sea from the Baltic was a permanent invitation to traders. The site does not even have to be uniquely propitious, provided it has seemed good enough to be chosen a first time. Kalisz, the oldest town in Poland, mentioned by Ptolemy, then by Pliny, then by the tenth-century traveler Ibrahim inb-Yaqub, lies on the bank of an undistinguished river, at an unremarkable point of the great Polish plain. But the ancient amber route at one time passed there, and this, it seems, was enough to establish Kalisz as the urban focus of an agricultural region that called for a town. Still, continuity of settlement does not necessarily mean continuity of urban activities; Lübeck was scarcely a city before its last reconstruction by Henry the Lion and the West German merchants he invited; Kalisz, even today, is hardly more than an overgrown village. Moreover, the already mentioned phenomenon of shifting commercial centers is more pronounced in non-Roman than in formerly Roman territories. Whatever urban life there was in early medieval Sweden favored little islands surrounded by the placid water of lakes; but the islands changed. The main center was Lillö in the seventh century, Birka in the ninth, Sigtuna in the eleventh, Stockholm by the thirteenth.

At any rate, if we agree with Alcaeus that what makes a city is men able to use their opportunity, the physical continuity of settlement matters less than the ideal continuity of the urban mind. Civilization, in the Latin vocabulary, literally meant "urbanization"; the difference between the elite and the mass, between the Roman and the barbarian, was tied to the fact that the former preferred gregarious living in towns, whereas the latter clung to isolated homesteads in the country. This distinction, however, was never absolute, and it became more blurred in the latter days of the Empire: the Roman aristocrats and intellectuals in droves quit the towns, made unpleasant by tax collectors and foreign invaders; the barbarians trickled into the Roman towns and learned their way of life. To some extent, the process continued after the fall of Rome: while many members of the old elite sought in the country an air uncontaminated by moral corruption and by un-Roman neighbors, the urban amenities captured most of the Gothic aristocrats, many of the Lombards, some Franks, and even a handful of Anglo-Saxon gentlemen. In the long run, however, it was inevitable that the conquerors shed their inferiority complexes and that the ideal of the polished citizen, conversing with fellow-citizens and buying sophisticated goods in citizens' shops, be superseded by the ideal of the sturdy baron, talking down to his table companions and getting from his serfs whatever goods the serfs might be able to produce.

What saved the town, in the early centuries of the early Middle Ages, was not so much the lay Roman tradition as the ecclesiastic tradition that had been grafted on it. If "civilization" originally meant "urbanization," "church" originally meant "gathering." Its administration, born under the Roman Empire, duplicated the pattern of civil government, with episcopal sees rooted in cities and archiepiscopal sees in the capitals of larger circumscriptions. To their cities, bishops brought a retinue and an income. They endeavored to maintain some order when lay government was inadequate, to bring food when it was lacking, and to do something about communications between the urban center and the rural parishes, which they were supposed to inspect periodically. And while today we may not automatically associate a gathering of clergymen with the highest dynamism, efficiency, and intellectual progressiveness, in the early Middle Ages these qualities could be found almost exclusively within the Church. The medieval legal convention that made city and episcopal see equivalent terms was then fully compatible with the notion that a city is at once a keeper of traditions and an accelerator of change.

Not only did the Church give a new lease on life to many old towns that might otherwise have disappeared, but it took over to some extent the practice of pegging its expansion to the foundation of towns. Thus, when Charlemagne conquered the land of the Saxons and forced the inhabitants to convert to Christianity, it was pointed out that "in that region there were absolutely no *civitates*, where episcopal sees might be established in conformity with ancient custom"; and his ecclesiastic and lay officials went to work to make up for the deficiency. The movement, slow at first, gathered momentum under the later Carolingians and still more under the Ottonian dynasty; a good proportion of the modern towns in northern and east central Europe trace their historical origins back to an early medieval bishopric, or another ecclesiastic establishment. It is true that in the peculiarly unsociable environment of Ireland, where Christianity had to make its way by persuasion rather than by force, the bishops were unable to introduce urban living. They merely dubbed *civitates* a number of monasteries, where only members of the clergy had to submit to a measure of disciplined togetherness; and there still were such stubborn individualists as the three monks who, in 891, "fled Ireland in an oarless ship because they wanted to live as pilgrims for the love of God."

Monasteries, at any rate, were cities of a sort, much as they proposed to steer people away from the contagion of metropolitan vice. If they usually contributed more to intellectual than to economic activities, if they depended heavily on tributes and services of agricultural laborers, the same had been true for many Roman cities, controlled by landowners. A good number of them were established just outside the walls of a pre-existing city, where a still enforced Roman hygienic rule confined all burial places, even if the bodies were relics of saints. In these cases, the monastery might attract enough settlers, partly by siphoning them away from the walled town, to grow into a new suburb. Other monasteries, such as Montecassino, Fulda, and Ely, arose in comparative isolation and gave impetus to new towns. Apart from the monastic kernel, there often was considerable social diversity. The abbey of St. Riquier, for instance, in the Carolingian period was flanked by several clusters of houses (*vici*), inhabited by merchants (*negotiatores*), smiths, shield-makers, saddlers, cobblers, furriers, fullers, wool carders, bakers, and "wine makers."

Next to the traditions and policy of the Church, the need for security was probably the most important factor in urban survival and, still more, revival. As a matter of fact, the need was least felt during the long lull between the German and Hunnic invasions that ushered in the so-called Dark Ages, and the Saracen, Norse, Magyar, and Slavic invasions that ushered them out. That period (almost three centuries) however unprofitable for intellectual endeavor, was one of the least war-ridden stretches in human history. Still, war was not unknown, and even in its absence, internal struggles and brigandage would remind people that there is safety in numbers, and that the ready-made walls of the late Roman Empire might some day prove their usefulness. Or, when the shrunken agglomeration was too small for its external walls, any old stone heap might help: so did the tomb of Caecilia Metella near Rome, and the amphitheater in whose deep bowl the entire population of Arles came to huddle. Old walls, however, gradually fell in disrepair, or were torn down by diffident rulers (as around 640, when Rothair destroyed all fortifications of the conquered Ligurian towns), or were claimed by the Church for its own use. At the beginning of the sixth century, already, Bishop Avitus of Lyons claimed that his city was "more efficiently defended by its suburban basilics than by its walls." By the early ninth century, there was a rash of French bishops tearing down urban walls to reuse their stones.

The timing could scarcely have been worse. Before the first round of demolitions was completed, a new tide of invasions brought down the Carolingian Empire and swept away all but the best fortified obstacles on its path. Ecclesiastic and lay lords then hastened to patch up or reconstruct walls and towers, often with the assistance of refugees from the country, who remained in the sheltered town after the emergency had passed. Sometimes it did not seem enough to restore the defensive works in the old location, especially if they had succumbed to a first attack, and the entire community — both the old residents and the newcomers — moved to higher ground in the vicinity. This was not entirely a new trend and was not determined exclusively by military considerations: the higher the hill, the less it was exposed to malaria, floods, and other whims of waters, over which the Romans had lost control, and the barbarians had never exercised any. Even the urban tradition of the Church had yielded, here and there, to such seeming acts of God: mosquitoes and enemy raids drove the bishop of Luni to the hill of Sarzana; the bishop of Anicium moved with his flock to the formidable rocks of Le Puy-en-Velay; the monks and laymen of Verulamium climbed a hilltop which they proclaimed the true site where St. Alban, their patron, was made a martyr.

By the tenth century, as the demographic trend reversed itself, as agriculture picked up, and as local forces rose to the challenge, new urban nodes also began to sprout around isolated hilltop castles and, beyond the former limits of Roman urbanistic civilization, around primitive villages of the eastern and northern European plains, where rivers and moats rather than rocks and slopes afforded protection. Soon, however, the choice of nearly inaccessible sites for urban settlement looked as inconvenient as the demolition of walls one century before; for easy access is a prime asset for a town, especially if it has to depend on trade for most of its food (some food being usually grown inside the town area) and for the exchange of its own artisan production with foreign handicraft and luxury goods. Antiquity had usually taken care of these opposite exigencies by combining an acropolis or capitol for defense and a forum and market for communication. Much in the same way, the reviving town of the later Middle Ages combined a fortified church or castle on high with, at its foot, a public square and market, soon to be known as a suburb. How the suburb outgrew the fortress and eventually merged with it, under the impulse of growing trade, is not within our chronological scope.

The story cannot be left at this point, however, without mentioning that the combination of castle and suburb, though most frequent in northern and eastern Europe and not unknown in the south, was by no means a universal feature of town development in the age of the Commercial Revolution (from the tenth to the fourteenth century). Some of the ancient towns, depressed though they were, preserved throughout and beyond the "Dark Ages" the main lines of their physical and social structure. Here, whatever dualism between acropolis and market may have originally existed had been blurred in the golden age of Roman urbanism; the elements had remained interlocked ever since; and the new age of growth saw them expand jointly. Milan is the outstanding example, though only one of many. The flat, riverless soil never permitted Milan to have an acropolis or an island fortress; so far as we can tell from a meager and sometimes discontinuous record, traders and artisans always rubbed shoulders with lay and ecclesiastic officials in the center of the town. And while we must assume that many buildings were destroyed or changed their destination, we keep hearing of certain focal points, which may have shifted somewhat, but remained substantially close to one another: the main public place, the public mint, the main public market, embellished by a royal hall or pavilion, and surrounded by houses of merchants and craftsmen. All of them were in the same general area where the central square, the main banks, and the best shops are still located today.

Let us go back to trade, once again, before concluding. It is not without significance that in modern Milan the largest bank is on approximately the same spot as the early medieval mint, and that a portion of the area of the early medieval market is now called Via Mercanti and occupied by some of the world's most elegant shops. But it is evident that today's shops cannot possibly be very similar to those of the sixth, or eighth, or tenth century; nor are they all concentrated in the old market area. We must not yield to the temptation of assuming that business went on as usual only and always when and where the meager sources mention familiar names of tradesmen (*negotiatores, fabri, carpentarii,* etc.) or of municipal officials (*curiales, notarii,* or merely *cives*). Silence is no proof of inexistence; if a town survived at all, we may take for granted that it had merchants and artisans of some sort, whether or not they are specifically mentioned. On the other hand, names change meaning; no city and no citizens could have endured but at the price of continuous adjustment.

This adjustment cannot be described in detail, but its main features are obvious enough, though they are not equally prominent in every town. Self-government and individual freedom, already threatened during the last centuries of the Roman Empire, deteriorated further; by the time of Gregory of Tours it was possible for a haughty count to pretend that a craftsman wandering in the streets of the town could be no other than a runaway serf; soon after, the last residual functions traditionally entrusted to *curiales* and other municipal officials faded away. Again, the characteristic symbiosis of a town specialized in commerce and industry with its district specialized in agriculture was loosened and blurred; the town, cut off from the country, endeavored to produce on its own soil some of the food it could no longer obtain by exchange for non-edible materials and manufactured wares. If trade, freedom, and self-government entirely vanished, the town became practically undistinguishable from a village or a manor; the mere fact that it may still have borne the name of *civitas* would then not be enough to keep it in our context. But a large number of towns yielded without surrendering, and saved whatever could be saved of urban life, chiefly by leaning upon their masters and main citizens, the ecclesiastic and military upper class.

What did a *negotiator*, a merchant, do for a living? He knew that the bishop, the abbot, the count, the margrave (often the bishop and the count were the same person) with their subordinates and vassals were his most dependable customers; theirs was most of the money and land, the greatest appetite, the keenest awareness of desirable goods a poorer and less mobile man might never have heard of. It was essential for a sedentary or quasi-sedentary merchant to establish the closest connection with the lord of his town — as a vassal, if he was that lucky, but even as a serf, if needed, for a serf trading with a bishop was usually better off than a free merchant trading with ordinary free men. In Arras, Tournai, Worms, and other northern towns, certain privileged serfs or semi-serfs (*censuales*) of churches and monasteries were the backbone of the merchant class, later to be regarded as the elite of the bourgeoisie. They, and other merchants who acted as sales managers and purveyors to ecclesiastic and lay institutions, often shared with their masters some special rights and immunities that also covered their own private transactions. The status of a merchant, however, did not have to be humble. In some Italian towns, we come across free *negotiatores* who had vassals of their own and sat at the side of the judges in the Carolingian courts. By the tenth century, they might wax as exalted as one Bariberto of Como, to whom Otto III donated land and a section of the town walls near the estates he already owned. In turn, a merchant of Regensburg in 983 donated to an abbey several plots of land within the city and outside.

If a *negotiator* did not confine his business to one town and one district, but engaged in long-distance commerce, he could more easily maintain his independence. No matter whether he carried prestige-giving silks and jewels or indispensable salt and grain, it was in the interest of all lords he served that his movements be untrammeled and protected. He might be entrusted with delicate diplomatic missions, as were Liutfred of Mainz (the "opulent merchant") and Dominic of Venice, whom Emperor Otto the Great made his ambassadors to the emperors Constantine VII and Nicephorus Phokas. Indeed, one reason for the spectacular rise of Venice, Amalfi, and other Italian towns along the borders of three mutually hostile civilizations (Catholic, Greek, and Muslim) was the general need for middlemen who would maintain commercial intercourse even in time of war. Each belligerent power granted them privileges, accepting their tokens of allegiance at face value, and ignoring similar tokens they simultaneously gave the other powers. Less spectacularly, but still in open defiance of legal and religious standards, the "most honorable . . . mightily rich" Christian merchants of Verdun took to Muslim Spain herds of slaves purchased or captured in many countries, and, on their way

back, appeased their conscience by buying illegally the relics of a
saint and bringing them home to work miracles in behalf of their
fellow-citizens. Still better off, in spite of legal disabilities, were
the Jewish merchants, whose standards and allegiance were every-
where rejected, but whose services were universally welcome
through the back door. All the curses of Agobard, the bishop of
Lyons, did not prevent them from eclipsing all other merchants
of his city, under the protection of their most illustrious client,
Emperor Louis the Pious.

Yet, in the long run, the disabilities of the Jews were to prove a
stumblingblock. Citizenship never ceased to be an asset, nor did
urban communities ever lose every bit of self-government. When
bishops and counts took over nearly all the functions formerly belonging to municipal bodies and magistrates, they still left some
petty matters in care of ordinary residents: the lowest forms of
legal certification and debate, the administration of common land,
public health and road repair, sometimes local defense. In Italy,
as early as 750, King Aistulf singled out the merchants for general
military service on horse or foot, according to their wealth; in
France, by 877, Charles the Bald bestowed upon the "negotia-
toribus vel qui in civitatibus commanent" the dubious honor of
paying a special quota of the tribute to the Normans. Little by
little, class distinctions emerged within the merchant community
(in Italy, "maiores et potentes, sequentes, minores" as early as
750; in Arras, 879, "nobiliores, inferiores, pauperes"; and so forth),
and the whole community reached for greater power. We do not
know what was behind the "malevolent conspiracy of the people"
which temporarily threw out the bishop of Turin in 897, but con-
spiracies against the lord became commonplace in tenth-century
Italy, and by 958 there is a *coniuratio* against the bishop even in
the northern town of Cambrai. All these may have been tumultuary actions, perhaps arising from overexcited sessions of the *con-
ventus ante ecclesiam*, the open-air meetings in the yard of the
cathedral.

The assemblies, however, did not have forever to be tumultuary.
In 971, what we might call the earliest surviving written report of

a medieval town meeting shows a most orderly parliament in Venice — the doge, the patriarch, and several bishops, sitting down; the rest of the people, "that is, the higher, the middle, and the lower," standing in their presence — which debates vital problems of commercial politics, and issues a decree sworn to by the entire attendance. In 998, the people of Cremona, long engaged in a methodical struggle against the episcopal tolls hitting their merchant barges, issue their orders from a town hall of their own. The early Middle Ages have gone; the age of free cities and merchant princes is around the corner.

᙮ JOSEPH R. STRAYER ᙮

THE TWO LEVELS OF FEUDALISM

FEUDALISM is one of the oldest interests of medievalists; its study goes back to the seventeenth century. Books on feudal institutions rank high among the classics of medieval historiography, from the pioneering work of Brussel and Madox in the early eighteenth century [1] to the well-known studies by Bloch, Haskins, Mitteis, and Stenton in the first half of the twentieth century.[2] One would think that the subject is now exhausted. But a new generation of scholars is revising and refining some of our earlier concepts through a more careful study of local history and a more precise dating of successive stages of development. We are, I hope, closer than ever before to understanding what feudalism was, how it developed, why it was significant.

What was feudalism? The men who first used the word (late seventeenth or early eighteenth century) were perfectly clear about its meaning. Feudalism was a type of government in which political power was treated as a private possession and was divided

---

[1] Brussel, *Nouvel examen de l'usage général des fiefs,* 2 vols. (Paris, 1727); T. Madox, *Baronia Anglica* (London, 1741).

[2] Marc Bloch, *La société féodale,* 2 vols. (Paris, 1949), English tr. L. A. Manyon (London and Chicago, 1961); C. H. Haskins, *Norman Institutions* (Cambridge, Mass., 1925); H. Mitteis, *Lehnrecht und Staatsgewalt* (Weimar, 1933); F. M. Stenton, *The First Century of English Feudalism* (Oxford, 1932).

among a large number of lords.[3] In spite of all the arguments
about the subject since, this is still the best definition. If we make
it broader and try to base our definition on economic and social
conditions, we soon find that we have defined nothing. To say, for
example, that the essence of feudalism is the exploitation of the
tillers of the soil by a politically dominant class is to throw together into one category societies as diverse as those of ancient
Rome, imperial China, medieval France, eighteenth-century England, and even the Soviet Union. In fact, a collective farm is in
some ways more like a European medieval manor than a European medieval manor was like a medieval Chinese village. The fact
of exploitation is unfortunately too common in history to serve as
a very useful tool in analyzing societies. What is important is the
method and degree of exploitation, or the origin and end result of
a period of exploitation. Here the differences among societies are
more significant than the resemblances and we do not help our
thinking by using the word "feudalism" to cover over these differences.

At the other extreme is the narrow, military definition of feudalism: it is a way of raising an army of heavy-armed cavalrymen
by uniting the two institutions of vassalage and the fief. This is a
good definition as far as precision goes. It applies only to Western
Europe in the Middle Ages; even the case of Tokugawa Japan
(the nearest possible parallel) does not fit exactly. The trouble is
that it is too limited. It focuses attention on only one aspect, and
that not the most important aspect, of feudalism. In fact, one
could argue that feudalism as a military system was a failure, that
the very union of vassalage and the fief in which some experts see
the essence of feudalism inevitably led to a rapid withering away
of the vassal's military value to his lord. Certainly the complete
union of vassalage and the fief does not take place until after 900,

[3] Brussel, *Nouvel examen de l'usage général des fiefs*, I, xlix, ". . . la pleine
connoissance de l'usage général des fiefs au tems de ces trois siècles (1000–1300)
emporte avec elle celle des maximes du gouvernement de toute la France." Bloch,
La société féodale, I, 3, remarks a little querulously that early writers "tenaient le
morcellement de la souveraineté entre une multitude de petits princes ou même de
seigneurs de village pour la plus frappante singularité du moyen âge. C'était ce
caractère qu'en prononçant le nom de féodalité ils croyaient exprimer."

and before 1100 every lord with any pretensions to military power is trying to supplement the services of his vassals by such devices as the hiring of mercenaries or the raising of urban or rural militias.[4] If feudalism were simply this brief and unsuccessful experiment in military organization, it would have little historical significance.

It was, of course, much more than this. What persisted, what left a deep impression on Western Europe, were feudal institutions of government and feudal concepts of law. Crude at first, these institutions and their concepts showed a surprising capacity for growth. The regions of Europe which were the most thoroughly feudalized (by any definition) were the regions that eventually developed the governments which became the models for all other European states. There are few basic institutions of European governments of the early modern period which did not first appear in the French or English monarchies of the Middle Ages. And it was precisely in northern France and in England after the Conquest that feudalism reached its fullest development. English and French government, English and French law grew out of feudal courts and out of problems of feudal relationships.

For the purposes of this essay, then, we shall take feudalism to mean a type of government which was conspicuous in Western Europe from about 900 to 1300 and which was marked by the division of political power among many lords and by the tendency to treat political power as a private possession. We shall consider the origins of this unusual political situation and follow its development down to the point at which the fragmentation of political power reached its maximum extent. We shall concentrate on France, because it was in France that feudalism developed first and most rapidly.

The task of seeking the origins of feudalism is complicated by

[4] J. O. Prestwick, "War and Finance in the Anglo-Norman State," *Transactions of the Royal Historical Society*, Series 5, IV (1954), 453–487; H. G. Richardson and G. O. Sayles, *The Governance of Mediaeval England* (Edinburgh, 1963), pp. 46–47, 70–83. Both authors state the case rather strongly, but even allowing for exaggeration it is perfectly clear that it would have been difficult to raise an effective army simply by demanding service from vassals who held fiefs.

the fact that feudalism existed on two levels, the level of the armed retainers who became feudal knights and the level of the royal officials (counts and their deputies, and *vassi dominici*) who became rulers of feudal principalities, counties, and castellanies. This is not to say that the two levels never mixed — no class distinction is ever that sharp or effective. It is also not to say that all retainers became knights or that all knights were descended from the old class of retainers. Some retainers were unable to qualify or to maintain themselves as knights, and some descendants of Carolingian officials (younger sons, heirs of dispossessed counts, and the like) were no more than knights. But it will simplify the discussion if we take the knights as typical of the lower level of feudalism and the counts as typical of the upper level.

On the whole the two levels were sharply separated both in social standing and in function during the early feudal period, say to about 1000. Even when the line between them became somewhat blurred, as it did in the eleventh and twelfth centuries, there was still an enormous difference between a simple knight and a great lord. Generalizations about one level do not always apply to the other level, especially during the formative period. And until there had been some integration of the two levels — specifically, until the lower level had acquired some political responsibilities and power — we do not have the full development of feudalism as a system of government.

Looking first at the lower level, we find that we can trace its origins far back in time. The armed retainer is an old figure in European history; he appears in Germany long before the migrations and in the Roman Empire long before its collapse in the West.[5] It is easy to see why he became more and more important as the institutions of the Roman Empire withered away. The process is especially clear in the Frankish kingdom. Kings who could not be sure of the loyalty or military competence of many of their subjects needed men bound especially to them to form the nucleus of their armies. Powerful men, or men who sought power, needed

[5] A good treatment of these early retainers is in P. Guilhiermoz, *Essai sur l'origine de la noblesse en France* (Paris, 1902), pp. 5–37.

54

bodyguards. The introduction in the eighth century of new military tactics, based on heavy-armed cavalry,[6] made it even more essential for the great men of the Frankish realm to secure the services of retainers. The ordinary subject or dependent could not afford the specially bred horses, the armor, and the years of training which made a good cavalryman. So the value of retainers, armed and trained in the new fashion, rose. It is at this time that they begin to gain a virtual monopoly of the appellations "vassal" and "miles" or knight. Originally a vassal had been any kind of retainer and a "miles" any kind of soldier. But now *the* vassal, *the* soldier, was the heavy-armed cavalryman.

Kings and other important men naturally tried to make sure that they would always have the services of these expert soldiers. They bound their retainers to themselves for life by solemn oaths and by the ceremony of homage. They gave them lavish gifts of jewelry, fine clothes, and weapons. Very early — even before 800 — some vassals were granted lifetime possession of revenue-producing properties (usually landed estates) for their support.[7] During the ninth and tenth centuries most, but not all, vassals received such grants. When this practice had become common we have that union of vassalage (retainership) and the fief (the gift of land) which many scholars have claimed is the essence of feudalism.

The difficulty with this assertion is that the retainers who became vassals had no political power. They were, in many cases, not even free men. The Celtic word "vassal" had originally meant servant, just as had the Anglo-Saxon word "knight." [8] In the post-Carolingian period in Germany and in the eastern region of France there were many knights who were not free.[9] Even in Nor-

[6] A convenient summary of earlier literature on the subject and a very strong statement about the importance of the change in tactics may be found in L. T. White, *Medieval Technology and Social Change* (Oxford, 1962), pp. 2–14, 26–38.

[7] F. L. Ganshof, *Qu'est-ce que la féodalité?* (Neuchatel, 1947), English tr. Philip Grierson (London, 1952), pp. 51–61, and more fully, "L'origine des rapports féodo-vassaliques," *I Problemi della Civiltà Carolingia*, Settimane di Studio del Centro Italiano di Studi sull'Alto Medioevo I (Spoleto, 1954), pp. 46ff.

[8] Guilhiermoz, *Essai sur l'origine de la noblesse en France*, pp. 55–57; Bloch, *La société féodale*, I, 239–240, 281–282.

[9] F. L. Ganshof, "Étude sur les ministeriales en Flandre et en Lotharingie,"

mandy — a region which had almost no serfs — the duke in a document issued just before the Conquest found it necessary to specify that he was speaking of "free knights."[10]

Perhaps in France a majority of the knights were free, but they were not noble. Here we must be careful to avoid confusion. As was said above, the ordinary Latin word for knight was "miles." But "miles" was also used as a synonym for "vassal," even for a vassal of high rank.[11] It was also used as a title by men who were building up semi-independent lordships, men who would eventually rank as barons.[12] Thus many nobles might be called "milites" but this does not mean that all "milites" were noble. Recent studies have demonstrated conclusively that in most areas the ordinary knight was not considered noble until the late twelfth or even the thirteenth century.[13]

This is important because of the profoundly aristocratic nature of the Carolingian and post-Carolingian periods. Only nobles were supposed to rule and the vast majority of knights were thus outside the ruling class. Down to 1000 political power was concentrated in the hands of a very small group — counts and a few of their chief subordinates. Ordinary knights were not seigneurs; they did not have courts or the right to command and to punish.

Knights did not even participate, to any marked extent, in the governmental activities of their superiors. Before 1000 it is rare to

Mémoires de l'Academie royale de Belgique, classe des lettres, 2nd series, XX (1926); M. Bloch, "La ministérialité en France et en Allemagne," *Revue historique de droit français et étranger*, 1928, pp. 46–91; G. Duby, "La noblesse dans la France mediévale," *Revue historique*, CCXXVI (1961), 15.

[10] Marie Fauroux, *Recueil des actes des ducs de Normandie* (Caen, 1961), no. 199. The document is dated by the editor 1051–1066.

[11] F. L. Ganshof, "Les relations féodo-vassaliques aux temps post-Carolingiens," *I Problemi Comuni dell'Europa Post-Carolingia*, Settimane di Studio del Centro Italiano di Studi sull'Alto Medioevo II (Spoleto, 1955), pp. 83–84.

[12] Karl F. Werner, "Untersuchungen zur Fruhzeit des französischen Fürstentums," *Die Welt als Geschichte*, XIX (1959), 170, 185 (other portions of this remarkable article appeared in the same journal in 1958 and 1960); A. Bernard and A. Bruel, *Recueil des chartes de l'abbaye de Cluny* (Paris, 1876–1903), no. 3278, Acelin "miles de Masco," early eleventh century.

[13] Much of this work is summed up in G. Duby, "La noblesse," pp. 1–6, 14–18. See also Werner, in *Die Welt als Geschichte*, XIX (1959), 185–187, XX (1960), 117–119.

find a simple knight witnessing the acts of his lord, much less acting as an adviser or a judge in his court. Witnesses and judges came from a higher level — members of the count's own family, bishops and abbots who were almost all members of the great noble families, viscounts, castellans, and the like.[14] Only when the fragmentation of political power reached its peak in the eleventh century did lords find it necessary to call in knights to help them make their judgments.[15] In short, down to 1000 the group of vassals descended from the old class of retainers had little to do with feudalism as a form of government.

The upper level of feudalism was something entirely different. The men who participated in this level came from the old Frankish aristocracy — an aristocracy which had a virtual monopoly of all high offices in the realm, and especially of the office of count. In the early years of the Frankish kingdom a few men of low birth had been made counts — even then much to the disgust of the ar-

[14] G. Duby, "Récherches sur l'évolution des institutions judiciaires pendant le X⁰ et XI⁰ siècle," *Le Moyen Age*, XLII (1946), 154–155; Fauroux, *Actes des ducs de Normandie*, pp. 58–62; Werner, in *Die Welt als Geschichte*, XIX (1959), 186. Ordinary knights never witness acts of Robertians and, as J. F. Lemarignier points out, when the Capetian descendants of the Robertians began to use knights as witnesses in the early eleventh century it marked a decline in their position ("Structures monastiques et structures politiques de la France de la fin du X⁰ et des debuts du XI⁰ siècle," *Il Monachismo nell'Alto Medioevo*, Settimane di Studio del Centro Italiano di Studi sull'Alto Medioevo IV [Spoleto, 1957], pp. 365–367).

[15] A few examples from different regions will demonstrate the point; many more could be given:

Flanders: B. Guérard, *Polyptyque de l'abbé Irminon* (Paris, 1844), II, 357 (six knights witness an act of 1038 and "hoc placitum fecerunt quatuor milites advocati").

Burgundy: Duby, "Institutions judiciaires," pp. 177, 192; and Bernard and Bruel, *Chartes de Cluny*, no. 3262 (four knights of Cluny "fecerunt placitum," mid-eleventh century).

Hainaut: L. Génicot, "Le premier siècle de la curia de Hainaut," *Le Moyen Age*, LIII (1947), 48 (knights are part of *curia* soon after 1050).

Provence: Georges de Manteyer, *La Provence du 1ᵉʳ an 12⁰ siècle* (Paris, 1908), pp. 279, 281 (after the 1020's the count gets consent of *fideles* or *milites*).

Normandy, Fauroux: *Actes des ducs de Normandie*, nos. 107 (a ducal act approved by "omnibus suis militibus," 1046–1048), 13 (knights act as witnesses of an act of a count of Ivry, 1011), 16 (knights confirm an act of a count of Mortain, c.1015).

Anjou: L. Halphen, *Le comté d'Anjou au XI⁰ siècle* (Paris, 1906), p. 109 (the count founds a church "cum consilio hominum meorum in ipso castro habitantium," some of the "men" are minor vassals, 1006–1021).

istocracy — but by the time of Charlemagne this practice had ended. And, given the simple administrative structure of the Frankish Empire, the counts were the government as far as most inhabitants were concerned. A count had full judicial, financial, and military power in the *pagus* or *pagi* which he ruled. His behavior was checked from time to time by inspectors sent out from the royal court (the *missi*), but only in the most extreme cases of misbehavior or disobedience was there much chance that a count's decision would be reversed or that he would lose his office. Men of the count's own class could lodge complaints against him in the king's court, but there was little danger that an ordinary freeman would take such a step. And the office gave profit as well as power — a share in the fines levied in the local courts and the possession of estates attached to the countship. It is not surprising that the great Frankish noble families sought to accumulate as many countships as they could.

Under Charlemagne, and throughout most of the ninth century, countships were not hereditary. Nevertheless, there was a strong tendency to keep countships in the same families. There was no rule of primogeniture, and a connection on the mother's side counted just as much as one on the father's side, so that relationships are not always easy to discover. But most ninth-century counts whose descent we can trace were related in some way to men who had held the same countships before them.[16]

This does not mean, however, that members of the great Frankish families quickly took root in specific regions, or that their first aim was to set up semi-independent local lordships. There were relatively few families in the upper aristocracy and there had been extensive intermarriage among them. Thus most men who could hope for the office of count had relatives, and therefore claims to office, in many parts of the Empire. Even more important, while it was pleasant and profitable to rule a single county, it was even better to hold the office of duke or marquis which gave control of many counties. These offices, established as great commands for

[16] Duby, "La noblesse," pp. 6, 11–12; Werner, in *Die Welt als Geschichte*, XX, 102.

the defense of frontier areas, could be acquired only through the special favor of the king. The leaders of the aristocratic families therefore formed factions which intrigued at the royal court for possession of the great commands. The triumph of one faction and the disgrace of another regularly caused shifts in the great commands and quite often shifts in the countships subordinated to those commands.[17] Thus regional concentrations of power in the hands of one man were at first impermanent and unstable. They depended on family connections and on successful political maneuvering at court more than on possession of local offices and lands.

The great families remained quite mobile well into the ninth century. Lesser aristocrats, the men who were deputies and aides of the counts, took root more rapidly, although even these men moved about rather freely in the eighth and early ninth centuries. When they did settle down they had little independent power; they remained subordinates of whoever held the county.

Events of the ninth and early tenth centuries sharply decreased the mobility of the aristocracy. The Empire broke up into kingdoms which were often hostile to one another. At first the great nobles still moved freely from kingdom to kingdom, but this became more difficult as divisions hardened and rivalries sharpened. Civil wars weakened the power of the kings, especially in the west Frankish realm. This meant that court intrigue became less useful as a means of securing high office, since it was by no means certain that the king's orders granting such offices would be obeyed. At the same time new waves of invasion, especially those of the Northmen, further weakened the unity of the Frankish kingdoms and the authority of their kings. The west Frankish kings, in particular, were not very successful in repelling invaders and the aristocracy had to take much of the responsibility for defense. A family which had fought to defend a group of counties acquired a vested interest in that area, and people there began to regard members of such a family as their natural, hereditary rulers.

In short, during the ninth and early tenth centuries, members

[17] Werner, in *Die Welt als Geschichte*, XIX, 150–169.

of the great aristocratic families began to take root in specific regions.[18] In a world which was falling apart this seemed to be the best way to preserve their wealth, their standard of living, and their pre-eminent political position. And because royal power was declining so rapidly in France, in that kingdom the great men became rulers of large, virtually independent principalities. The king had no power to correct or review governmental acts which took place within their principalities; political power had become a private, hereditable property for great counts and dukes.

Several of the principalities, in turn, proved to be too large or too loosely organized to be governed by one man. They included many *pagi*, too many for a duke, marquis, or "super-count" to rule directly. The head of a principality had to have deputies (subordinate counts or viscounts) to act for him in different parts of his holdings. Theoretically, there should have been one deputy for each *pagus*; in practice most of the subordinate counts and some of the abler viscounts acted in several *pagi*. These men, drawn from the lesser aristocracy, were quite capable of becoming independent. They ruled fairly sizable territories, had numerous vassals of their own, and were often neglected by their distant superiors. Thus subordinate counts of the duke of Burgundy, such as the count of Auxerre, shook off all control from above. The viscounts of the Robertian dukes of the Loire-Seine region, such as the viscount of Anjou, soon took the title of count and became equally independent. The dukes of Normandy were almost unique in their ability to keep their subordinate counts and their viscounts from setting up autonomous lordships.

Down to the year 1000, however, the process of disintegration usually stopped at this point. The *pagus* remained the smallest unit of government and political power remained concentrated in a very restricted group of counts, viscounts, and men of equivalent rank and standing.

I have deliberately described the growth of the power and inde-

[18] *Ibid.*, XX, 119, speaks of "der Übergang vom fluktuierenden Adel des 8. und 9. Jahrhunderts zum fixierten Adel des 10. und 11." See also the very important work of J. Dhondt, *Études sur la naissance des principautés territoriales en France* (Bruges, 1948), especially pp. 231ff.

pendence of the counts and other members of the aristocracy without relating it to the rise of the class of knights. There were connections between the two processes, but it is by no means evident that one development could not have taken place without the other. Given ninth-century conditions — an agrarian economy, poor communications, destructive invasions — the chances of survival of a great empire, or even of a large kingdom, were poor; political fragmentation would have occurred whether knights had existed or not. Since knights did exist, counts used them in their armies, but they would have needed private armies in any case. Conversely, given the state of military technology in the ninth century, a class of heavy-armed cavalrymen would have developed even if there had been no political fragmentation. In fact, the first great steps toward creating a knightly class were taken when the Carolingian rulers were at the height of their power, and the knights had no inherent objections to serving kings rather than counts. They would fight for anyone who would reward them; it was simply the weakening and impoverishment of the kings which gave the aristocracy the opportunity to acquire the services of most of the knights.

Though the two levels of feudalism remained quite distinct down to 1000 (and even beyond), the difference between them was obscured by a confusion in terminology. The same words were used to describe two very different types of relationship. And this confusion goes back to a deliberate decision of the Carolingian kings. These kings were quite aware that there were fundamental weaknesses in their position, that the bond between king and subject was becoming increasingly tenuous, that local government was monopolized by the aristocracy. They saw on the other hand that the bond between vassal and lord was strong and effective. They therefore tried to create the same ties between themselves and the aristocracy which existed between the aristocracy and the lesser vassals. While great men were seldom called vassals,[19] they

[19] Here the basic study is Charles E. Odegaard, *Vassi and Fideles in the Carolingian Empire* (Cambridge, Mass., 1945). It is interesting to note that down to 1066 the Norman dukes almost never use the word "vassallus"; the two exceptions in 1059 and 1063 (Fauroux, *Actes des ducs de Normandie*, nos. 142, 156) are in

were asked to do homage and take vows of fidelity to the king, just
as a vassal did homage and swore fidelity to a lord. At the same
time the kings began to speak of the conferring of a high office
(such as a countship) as the bestowal of a "benefice" (that is, a
fief).[20] In short, there was an apparent parallel between the relationship of a knight to a lord and the relationship of a count to a
king.

In the long run, a very long run, this policy proved useful. In
the twelfth and thirteenth centuries French kings were able to re-
establish their power over the rulers of feudal principalities by in-
sisting that these men owed obedience and service as vassals. But
this was in a very different social and political context. As far as
the Carolingians were concerned, their policy was an almost complete failure. There was a tremendous difference between the binding force of homage and fidelity on an ordinary knight and that on
a member of a great aristocratic family. The knight was nothing
by himself — he had no prestige, no political power, not even (as
an individual) much military significance. He had to have a lord
to function effectively; he had to serve the lord frequently and
faithfully because he had no importance except as a member of a
group acting under the lord's direction. The member of a great
aristocratic family, on the other hand, was either a count himself,
or was related to a large group of counts, bishops, abbots, and
other lords. He had large estates, loyal retainers, and an assured
social position. Such a man was self-sufficient; he gave loyalty and
service only when he thought it was to his advantage to do so. The
fact that he had done homage to a king (or to one of the great
counts or dukes) merely established a certain bias in favor of ne-
gotiation rather than open defiance or war. Homages among the
great were more like treaties of nonaggression than contracts for
service.[21] Thus while both knights and counts might do homage

---

acts in favor of a non-Norman abbey, St. Julien de Tours. See also Ganshof, "Rélations féodo-vassaliques aux temps post-Carolingiens," p. 83, about the infrequent
use of "vassal" in France.

[20] Ganshof, "L'origine des rapports féodo-vassaliques," pp. 48, 61–62.

[21] An extreme example is provided by the *hommage en marche*; see J. F. Lemarignier, *Récherches sur l'hommage en marche* (Lille, 1945). Ganshof, "Rélations féodo-vassaliques," pp. 78–81, points out that the basic obligation, down to

and swear fealty, the reasons for and the results of the act were quite different.

The eleventh century saw the first moves toward a real (as opposed to a verbal) assimilation of the two levels of feudalism. It was in this century, as we have already seen, that knights began to be more prominent in the courts of their lords, witnessing charters, and acting as advisers and judges. It was also in this century that the *pagus* began to disintegrate as an administrative and judicial unit.[22] In many *pagi* the powers of the count or viscount were divided among a group of castellans who had rights of justice and command over the district immediately surrounding their castles.[23] The number of castellans tended to increase and those who were late in gaining this rank often had very small districts under their rule. The castellans, for the most part, were descended from the least important families of the old aristocracy, but they had more power and more independence than their ancestors had ever possessed. And as men of this class gained a certain degree of political authority it was not difficult to take the next step and allow knights to command and judge peasants on their estates.

The speed and degree of fragmentation varied greatly from region to region. In Normandy, for example, most of the *pagi* remained intact; the viscounts functioned as agents of the duke and castellans were powerful only along the exposed southern fron-

the eleventh century, was negative, not to harm the man to whom homage was given. Or, as Duby puts it, in *La société aux XI* et XII* siècles dans la région mâconnaise* (Paris, 1953), p. 194, in the tenth and eleventh centuries, homage between "grands seigneurs" is "une simple garantie, un engagement à ne pas nuire," but "prêté par un petit noble à un puissant, c'est un dévouement véritable, un engagement à servir."

[22] J. F. Lemarignier, "La dislocation du pagus et le problème des consuetudines," *Mélanges d'histoire du Moyen Age dédiés à la mémoire de Louis Halphen* (Paris, 1951), pp. 401–410, and also his "Structures monastiques," pp. 369–372; P. Feuchère, "Essai sur l'évolution territoriale des principautés française," *Le Moyen Age*, LVIII (1952), 85–102; Jean Richard, *Les ducs de Bourgogne* (Paris, 1954), pp. 84–88.

[23] Almost every history of a French province shows the rise of the castellans after 1000; see the works cited above in footnote 22 and, as samples of the process elsewhere, M. Garaud, "Les circonscriptions administratives du comté de Poitou au X* siècle," *Le Moyen Age*, LIX (1953), 11–61 and especially 58–61; Halphen, *Le comté d'Anjou*, pp. 152–169; Manteyer, *La Provence*, pp. 366–367, 417–419; Duby, *La société . . . dans la région mâconnaise*, pp. 161–163, 185–189.

tier.[24] Yet even in Normandy there were many more lords with rights of justice at the beginning of the twelfth century than at the beginning of the eleventh. In southern Burgundy and in Provence fragmentation of political power went much further and the count's court had no more authority than that of many other lords.[25] But even where fragmentation was most extensive it would be wrong to assume that all vassals received a share of political power. Household knights without fiefs were still common, and other knights had such small fiefs that they had almost no one to command or to judge.[26]

However uneven the development of feudalism in the eleventh century was, it is clear that this was the decisive period in its history. It was then that feudal courts began to take their characteristic form, and then that the division of political power began to reach its peak. Most important of all, it was then that the two levels of feudalism began to merge, that instead of sharply separated classes of noble rulers and non-noble retainers we begin to get a continuous spectrum stretching from the knight with minimal rights of justice up through the castellans to the lords of the great feudal counties.[27]

It is this union of the two levels of feudalism, rather than the earlier union of vassalage and the fief, which seems to me the essential step in the development of feudal institutions. For while

[24] L. Musset, "Aux origines de la féodalité normande," *Revue historique de droit français et étranger*, 4° serie, XXIX (1951), 150; Lemarignier, "Structures monastiques," p. 371.

[25] Duby, "Institutions judiciaires," pp. 155–162, 180–194; Manteyer, *La Provence*, pp. 366–368, 417–418.

[26] Duby, "La noblesse," p. 16; Richard, *Les ducs de Bourgogne*, pp. 99–102; Ganshof, "Rélations féodo-vassaliques," pp. 89–90.

[27] This process, of course, took place at different times in different regions; e.g., the diffusion of rights of justice seems to have gone more rapidly in Lorraine than in Burgundy; compare Ch. E. Perrin, *Récherches sur la seigneurie rurale en Lorraine* (Paris, 1935), pp. 665–670, and Duby, "Institutions judiciaires," pp. 191–194. In Normandy ordinary knights did not have jurisdiction of their own in the eleventh century, but by the time the *Tres Ancien Coutumier* was written (end of the twelfth century) such jurisdiction was taken for granted: "Quilibet dominus habet placita sua et furta et dominationes suas in terris suis" (Ch. 59, p. 50, of the edition by E. J. Tardif). The example given to prove this rule deals with a rear-vassal who holds a single knight's fee.

the eleventh century did not see the creation of a complete and well-organized feudal hierarchy of ranks, powers, and possessions, it did see the creation of conditions which made it both essential and possible to establish such a hierarchy. On the one hand, fragmentation of political power had gone so far that the resulting confusion and insecurity threatened the possessors of power themselves. If external order and internal structure could not be imposed on the feudal groups, then possession of political power was going to mean very little. On the other hand, the number of men capable of taking part in the political process had enormously increased. They were still a small minority of the whole population, but they were more numerous and represented a wider variety of interests and talents than had the ruling group of the preceding period. This enlargement of the group which was politically active offered real opportunities to capable rulers; one has only to think of the role played by knights and other rear-vassals in the creation of the more successful twelfth-century governments.[28] Thus the combination of a difficult political problem with the emergence of a wider political constituency stimulated the development of feudal law and feudal institutions. It was in feudal courts of the new type that solutions were slowly hammered out for the problems of security, of conflicting and overlapping jurisdictions, of relationships among men at all levels of feudalism. And in solving these problems, the men of the new feudal age began not only to systematize feudalism,[29] but also to lay the foundations of the modern European state.

[28] J. R. Strayer, "The Development of Feudal Institutions in the Twelfth Century," in *Twelfth Century Europe*, ed. M. Clagett, G. Post, and R. Reynolds (Madison, Wisc., 1961), pp. 84, 86.

[29] *Ibid.*, pp. 82–84.

≥ ADOLF KATZENELLENBOGEN ≤

THE IMAGE OF CHRIST IN
THE EARLY MIDDLE AGES

A BOOK-COVER of the eleventh century, now in the Pierpont Morgan Library in New York, combines two representations of Christ (Figure 1).[1] In the upper half He is enthroned within a mandorla which creates an ideal sphere of existence for Him. He is accompanied by two Seraphim. This image is shaped after the vision Isaiah had of the Lord. The prophet saw the Lord "sitting upon a throne, high and lifted up" (Isaiah 6:1), and the Lord was attended by Seraphim, each one having six wings (Isaiah 6:2). In the lower half the crucified Christ is shown between the Virgin Mary and John the Disciple.

The book-cover with its two scenes has specific characteristics of both form and meaning. First of all, the figures are wrought in gilded sheets and thereby given a supernatural appearance. The

[1] Upper cover of Ms. 708. See Marvin Chauncey Ross, "An Eleventh Century English Bookcover," *Art Bulletin*, XXII (1940), 83ff.

I would like to thank the following institutions for providing photographs and giving me permission to use them for illustrations: D. Anderson, Rome: Figs. 3, 13; Bibl. Mediceo-Laurenziana, Florence: Figs. 4, 14; Bibl. Nationale, Paris: Figs. 8, 9, 15, 16; British Museum: Fig 2; National Museum of Ireland, Dublin: Fig. 7; Pierpont Morgan Library: Fig. 1; Staatl. Bibl., Bamberg: Figs. 17, 18; Stadtbibl., Trier: Figs. 11, 12; Stiftsbibl., St. Gall: Fig. 5; Universitätsbibl., Giessen: Fig 10; Walters Art Gallery: Fig. 6.

background is also gilded; furthermore, it is spun over by a delicate network of filigree and enriched by a pattern of precious stones. Because of all this the figures of the Crucifixion are removed from actual space.

Secondly, the figures are symbolically differentiated from one another by size. Thereby the importance of Christ is stressed. His seated figure is larger than the attending Angels and the Crucifix towers in size over the Virgin and John. There are also expressive distortions in the design of Christ. The hands of the seated Christ are strongly enlarged so that the gestures of blessing and of holding the book are powerfully emphasized. Likewise, the head, the arms, and the hands of the Crucifix are disproportionally large so that the upper part of His body is more definitely accentuated than the lower part.

Finally, the superposition of Christ in Majesty over Christ suffering death makes a fundamental theological idea visible. We may remember some passages in the New Testament which define the total essence of Christ. In the second Epistle to the Corinthians (13:4) Paul says: "For though He was crucified through weakness, yet He liveth by the power of God." In the Epistle to the Philippians (2:8–9) the apostle writes: "He humbled Himself and became obedient unto death, even the death of the cross; wherefore God also hath highly exalted Him." In the Book of Revelation (1:18) the Son of man Himself utters: "I am He that liveth and was dead, and behold, I am alive for evermore."

It is these two types of complementary images, Christ on the Cross and Christ in Majesty, which I would like to discuss. The examples I have chosen are by necessity few in number. They span the time from the fifth to the early eleventh century and will allow us at least a glimpse at the complexity and the often radical changes that occur in the representation of Christ during the early Middle Ages.

We shall see how in the Early Christian art of the Mediterranean regions more naturalistic and more abstract representations can occur simultaneously. This depends not only on the particular region where a work of art was created and its particular artistic tradition, but also to some degree on the specific formal and expressive aims of an individual artist.

In transalpine art of the eighth century we shall encounter representations of the two themes where human forms are reduced to ornamental arabesques. This is obviously the result of the fact that Christian art in many areas remained strongly determined by the abstract, nonrepresentational art of the migrating tribes that had settled in those regions. We shall have to ask ourselves: Is the transformation of the figure of Christ into an ornamental pattern always something negative as far as the meaning of His image is concerned, or not?

Owing to the endeavors of the Carolingian rulers an essentially new kind of style arose in the late eighth century and the ninth century. In spite of local variations, Carolingian art stands in strong contrast to the art of the immediately preceding era. Crucifixes and Crucifixion scenes regain more natural forms, their inherent possibilities to be fully explored in the succeeding centuries. The theme of Christ in Majesty gains a new complexity, but a complexity combined with great clarity because the figures and their ideographical relations can be rationally understood.

To begin with Crucifixion scenes: [2] Two reliefs to be dated about 430 make it evident how different in essence contemporaneous Early Christian works can be.

An ivory relief, now in the British Museum, represents next to the Suicide of Judas the event of the Crucifixion in a calm, restrained manner (Figure 2).[3] The bystanders are selected from the Gospel according to John. In their calmness the Virgin Mary and John are contrasted with the somewhat more impulsive posture of the soldier thrusting his spear (now broken off) into Christ's side.

The style remains in the classical tradition of Roman art. The proportions of the figures are natural. The drapery defines volumetric bodies. The attitudes of Mary and John reflect human dig-

[2] For a survey of representations of the Crucifixion, see Paul Thoby, *Le Crucifix des Origines au Concile de Trente* (Paris, 1959).

[3] See Ernst Kitzinger, *Early Medieval Art in the British Museum* (London, 1955), p. 100.

nity. Just by turning toward Christ, but without dramatic gestures or anguished postures, Mary and John accept Christ's self-sacrifice. Calmly Christ faces the beholder. All the figures exist three-dimensionally on a little stage.

Yet even within the confines of a still naturalistic representation a non-naturalistic element enters. The wound in Christ's side indicates that He is dead, but in contrast to Judas whose death is signified by his closed eyes, Christ's eyes are open. This apparent contradiction in the representation of Christ dissolves if one realizes that according to theological interpretation, Christ died as man while His Godhead remained inviolate. To quote just one passage in St. Augustine's *Enarrationes in Psalmos*: "But He who is God, who wanted to assume one person in man and with man, could neither diminish nor grow, neither die nor be resurrected. He is dead because of the infirmity of man, but as God He does not die . . . rightly we say: Christ is dead although His Godhead does not die." [4]

In sharp contrast to this relief stands a panel from the wooden doors of S. Sabina in Rome (Figure 3).[5] It was obviously carved by an artist of a different kind, one who was trained not in the classical tradition of Roman art, but in the unclassical tradition of a peripheral region of the empire. It is a much rougher work, to be sure. The physical beauty, the natural dignity of the human figure is not sought. The existence of figures in space is ambiguous. Yet already at this point we might ask ourselves whether the obvious lack of certain values is not replaced, and compensated for, by the appearance of other values of a different kind.

Here only Christ is shown between the two thieves. No witnesses are present. Thus the content of the scene is more restricted. Christ is stressed in importance by His symbolically larger size. Although the palms of the hands show nails, only the ends of the

[4] St. Augustine, *Enarratio in Psalmum XL*: "Ille autem qui Deus est, qui unam personam habere in homine et cum homine voluit, nec decrescere nec crescere potuit, nec mori nec resurgere. Mortuus est ex infirmitate hominis, caeterum Deus non moritur . . . sic recte dicimus: Mortuus est Christus, etsi divinitas ejus non moritur" (Migne, *Patrologia latina*, XXXVI, col. 455).

[5] Wolfgang Fritz Volbach, *Frühchristliche Kunst* (Munich, 1958), pp. 63–64.

cross-beams are represented, so that the three figures appear in the attitude of praying. They are seen against a patterned background. Its three gables might give the impression of house façades, were it not for the fact that the pattern of stones continues upward outside the three gables. This denotes in all likelihood some serious misunderstanding of the model the artist might have used. What is more significant, however, is the fact that the head of Christ, already stressed by its size and its elevated position, is further emphasized in importance by a triangular frame. The heads of the two thieves, on the other hand, are contained in the area below the lateral triangles. Why, we might ask, is the head of Christ given such special emphasis? The answer, I think, can be found in a statement of the first Epistle to the Corinthians (11:3): "and the head of Christ is God." This passage was interpreted by medieval theologians in relation to Christ's Godhead. It was one of the basic christological tenets that Christ combines in one person both Godhead and manhood. It is the head that was chosen as a symbol to denote Christ's divinity.[6] By strongly emphasizing Christ's head, the artist of the relief expresses the very idea that even in the moment of death Christ combines in His person both natures, Godhead and manhood.

The miniature in the Rabula Gospels, painted about 586, is a comprehensive narrative rendering of the event (Figure 4).[7] Christ is flanked by the two thieves, the good one on Christ's right side, bending his head toward Him. There are the witnesses mentioned in the Bible, Mary and John on one side, three holy women on the other side. There is Stephaton with the sponge of vinegar fixed to a reed, Longinus thrusting the spear, and the group of soldiers casting lots for Christ's tunic. The whole scene is set in an actual landscape with two hills suggested in the background. Christ is stressed in importance — not by size, for He is not larger than the thieves; but in contrast to the thieves He wears a long sleeveless garment and is nailed to a taller cross. More important, His head is par-

[6] See Ernst H. Kantorowicz, *The King's Two Bodies, A Study in Mediaeval Political Theology* (Princeton, N.J., 1957), pp. 70ff.

[7] Florence, Bibl. Mediceo-Laurenziana, Ms. Plut. I. 56, fol. 13a. See Aloys Grillmeier, *Der Logos am Kreuz* (Munich, 1956), pp. 2–15, 81ff.

Figure 1. Christ in Majesty — Crucifixion. (Book Cover,
Pierpont Morgan Library)

Figure 2. Suicide of Judas — Crucifixion. (Ivory, British Museum)

Figure 3. Crucifixion. (Detail of Doors of S. Sabina, Rome)

Figure 4. Crucifixion. (Rabula Gospels, Florence)

Figure 5. Crucifixion. (Gospel Book, St. Gall)

Figure 6. Fibula. (Walters Art Gallery)

Figure 7. Crucifixion. (National Museum of Ireland)

Figure 8. Crucifix. (Sacramentary of Gellone, Paris)

Figure 9. Crucifix. (Sacramentary of Charles the Bald, Paris)

Figure 10. Crucifix. (Cologne Gospels, Giessen)

Figure 11. Crucifixion. (Egbert Gospels, Trier)

Figure 12. Crucifixion. (Egbert Gospels, Trier)

Figure 13. Christ in Majesty. (Detail of Doors of S. Sabina, Rome)

Figure 14. Christ in Majesty. (Codex Amiatinus, Florence)

Figure 15. Christ in Majesty. (First Bible of Charles
the Bald, Paris)

Figure 16. Christ in Majesty. (Sacramentary of Charles
the Bald, Paris)

Figure 17. Christ in Majesty. (Gospel Book, Bamberg)

Figure 18. Christ in Majesty. (Gospel Book, Bamberg)

ticularly emphasized by a halo; and even more important, by being silhouetted against the sky. All the other heads are kept below the skyline. Thus even within a more naturalistic representation Christ's head is singled out in importance as it reaches into the sky up to the sun and the moon which flank the cross.

When an Irish monk represented in a Gospel book the Crucifixion about the middle of the eighth century he had in all likelihood a miniature of the type of the Rabula Gospels as a model before his eyes (Figure 5).[8] From such a prototype he took the group of Christ clad in a sleeveless garment and the men with the sponge of vinegar and the spear; but he added two Angels to the group.

Here a complete ornamental transformation of human forms has taken place. The composition is a surface pattern rather than a disposition of apparently three-dimensional figures in a seemingly three-dimensional space.

Now the figure of Christ is completely flattened out and covered with a complicated pattern of interlaced bands. The painter was obviously trained in an artistic tradition that took delight in the decorative exuberance of intertwining lines. A fibula, to be dated about 600, may illustrate this tradition (Figure 6).[9] One can well imagine how the artist translated Christ's robe into an equally lively pattern of interlaced bands. The result? A complete misunderstanding of a Mediterranean model by a northern artist, one might say. But upon closer inspection one can detect a striking difference between the irregular curved design of the bands in the lower part and the firm symmetrical design of the bands in the upper part. There is a corresponding contrast between the withered legs of Christ, which hang without any strength to one side and the strength of the head, frontally facing the beholder. It is the head that is furthermore stressed by the two Angels. Their presence at the Crucifixion is not mentioned in the Bible, but as heav-

[8] St. Gall, Stiftsbibl., Ms. 51, p. 266. See Johannes Duft and Peter Meyer, *The Irish Miniatures in the Abbey Library of St. Gall* (Berne-Lausanne, 1954), pp. 69ff, 100–101.
[9] Marvin Chauncey Ross, *Arts of the Migration Period in the Walters Art Gallery* (Baltimore, Md., 1961), p. 64.

enly beings they fulfill the function of stressing the Godhead of Christ. The lower part of Christ's body with the irregularities of the drapery pattern and the weakness of the legs may well symbolize His manhood. It is in the lower zone that the two tormentors are active.

An Irish bronze relief of the same time shows identical compositional elements (Figure 7) .[10] Again one is tempted to say: This is an awkward, primitive work of art, impressive in the ornamental intricacies of the design, but a failure as a credible representation of the Crucifixion. The bodies of the figures are misshapen, the proportions awkward. While it seems justified to mention all these deviations from, and transformations of, natural forms, one should not stop with such observations, I think, but rather ask: Has nothing been gained through the neglect and loss of all the elements of natural forms? Is there not also here an obvious contrast between the large, smooth, immobile mask of Christ's head, its eyes staring at the beholder, and the body covered with intricate and lively geometric patterns? Furthermore, is there no striking contrast between the greater plasticity of Christ's head and the flatness of His feet that are only incised? In addition, we can observe how the energetic contours of the Angels differ from the closed contours of the more static tormentors. There is a similar contrast between the ornamentalized wings of the Angels pushing upwards and the equally ornamentalized mantles of the tormentors hanging down. Finally, the Angels emphasize vividly the head of Christ by the sharp angles of their legs, while the curves formed by the contours of their inner wings and legs define a halo for Christ's head. In other words, the idea that the head of Christ symbolizes His Godhead is in all likelihood once again made evident just because of the abstract quality of a decorative style.

A miniature in the French Sacramentary of Gellone of the second half of the eighth century stresses the idea of Christ's two natures in a different way (Figure 8) .[11] Here Christ is as paper-thin

[10] Dublin, National Museum of Ireland. See Françoise Henry, *Irish Art in the Early Christian Period* (London, 1947), p. 122.

[11] Paris, Bibl. Nat., Ms. lat. 12048, fol. 143v.

as the Crucifix in the St. Gall Gospels. He lacks any physical reality. He wears only a loincloth reduced to a flat design of wiggly lines. The legs hang limply down. All this denotes His manhood. But this idea is now strengthened by the stream of blood drops that gush down from His breast wound. On the other hand, the Godhead of Christ seems more emphatically stressed by the two Angels. They are not static in their attitudes, but express directional energies. With the speed of birds they swoop toward Christ's head.

While a Merovingian miniature of this type conveys a very specific message, other contemporaneous miniatures are, and probably were, difficult to understand, whenever decorative predilection took precedence over intelligible meaning and/or poor draftsmanship affected the meaning.

Two adjoining miniatures from a mid-eighth-century Sacramentary may illustrate the first point.[12] The miniature on the left-hand page, although purely ornamental in character, still has a clear meaning. The golden cross framed by an arch can denote the idea that the cross is not only the instrument of Christ's self-sacrifice but also a symbol of His victory over death and sin. The Alpha and Omega suspended from the cross-beam refer to the eternity of Christ who says in the Book of Revelation (1:8): "I am Alpha and Omega, the beginning and the ending."

The cross-like design on the opposite page, on the other hand, is puzzling. In its center stands the Lamb of God, symbol of Christ who suffered death; but why are the cross-arms decorated with heraldic animals? The birds flanking the cross are time-honored symbols of the souls which seek salvation; but why do they gradually increase in size from bottom to top and why does the upper pair turn away from the cross?

A somewhat later miniature of a more timid and, therefore, questionable draftsmanship is also puzzling in its meaning.[13] Here

---

[12] Sacramentarium Gelasianum, Vatican Libr., Ms. Reg. lat. 316, fols. 131v, 132. See André Grabar and Carl Nordenfalk, *Early Medieval Painting from the Fourth to the Eleventh Century* (New York, 1957), illustration on p. 128.

[13] Letters of St. Paul, Würzburg, Universitätsbibl., Ms. Mp. theol., fol. 69, fol.

the Crucifix is shown above the Miraculous Draught of the Fishes. This combination does not defy explanation. The boat was interpreted as the Church and the fish are symbols of those to be saved.[14] Therefore, the salvation brought about by Christ's death is combined here with the idea of the salvation brought about by the Church. One can also understand the meaning of the birds perched on the horizontal cross-beam and facing Christ; but why are the two thieves suspended from the cross-arms, where they replace, as it were, the Alpha and Omega? One can understand that Angels rise toward the good thief; but why are birds rising toward the bad thief?

Under the impact of the Carolingian Renaissance a strong reaction against this kind of art took place. Charlemagne, we should remember, did not only revive the empire. Because of his endeavors education was furthered; literature flourished; the texts of classical authors were copied, as were illuminated manuscripts of antiquity; churches were shaped after Early Christian prototypes. No wonder then that also in religious painting the pendulum swung strongly back toward more clearly understandable representations.

Two miniatures of the ninth century may illustrate these new aims and achievements. An illuminated page in the Sacramentary of Charles the Bald still retains an interest in decorative intricacies, such as the arabesques of interlaced lines at the ends of the cross (Figure 9);[15] they are now combined with acanthus leaves of antique derivation; yet here the decorative elements no longer affect the design of the figure of Christ. Once again He is shaped as a beautiful human being. Like the representations of the Crucifix in the preceding century this miniature is derived from some Early Christian model, but the Carolingian artist no longer transforms the figure into a decorative, and at the same time in all likelihood

---

7a. See E. Heinrich Zimmermann, *Vorkarolingische Miniaturen* (Berlin, 1916), fig. 220a.

[14] See St. Ambrose, *Expositiones in Lucam*, IV: ". . . fluctuantes de infimis ad superna traducunt" (*Patrologia latina*, XV, col. 1718); ". . . ad navem Petri, hoc est, ad Ecclesiam" (*ibid.*, col. 1720).

[15] Paris, Bibl. Nat., Ms. lat. 1141, fol. 6v.

an ideographic, pattern. He gives the figure of Christ natural proportions. He models Christ's body by light and shade and thereby
suggests three-dimensional forms. He indicates the rib cage. He
makes the design of the loincloth dependent on the volume of the
body. Thus Christ has regained human dignity, but the idea that
even on the cross He combines manhood and Godhead in one person is no longer obvious. There is an upper sphere into which
Christ's head projects, but the two lateral busts are not Angels.
The two medallions represent *all' antica* the sun and the moon. It
is only the fact that Christ sheds His blood from the breast wound
while His eyes are open that suggests the idea of the two natures.

In a miniature from the Utrecht Psalter we find a more narrative and dramatic rendering of the event.[16] Sketched with quick,
nervous, and expressive pen strokes, the tormentors are emphasized in their physical activity, the Virgin Mary and John in their
intense mental anguish. Although immobile in their postures, the
two witnesses seem to vibrate inwardly because of the sheer en-
ergy of the design. Christ Himself has become small in relation to
the other figures.[17]

About the year 1000 we can witness an even wider exploration
of formal and expressive possibilities inherent in the Crucifixion.
Two German miniatures painted in Cologne during the first half
of the eleventh century exemplify a tendency toward the lyrical
and intimate. The softness of the brushwork adds to this effect.

In the Gundold Gospels Christ towers over the witnesses.[18] He
is already dead. His head is bent. He hangs calmly on the cross,
shedding His blood. The Virgin and John approach Him with re-

[16] Utrecht, Univ. Libr., Cod. 32, fol. 90r. See E. T. Dewald, *The Illustrations of
the Utrecht Psalter* (Princeton, N.J., 1933), pl. CXLII.

[17] Other miniatures in the same manuscript represent the Crucifixion in a variety of ways: historically, with Christ among Stephaton and Longinus (fol. 51v;
Dewald, *The Illustrations of the Utrecht Psalter*, pl. LXXXII); or among the
thieves and torturers (fol. 85v; pl. CXXXV); symbolically, by a cross and the
instruments of Christ's martyrdom (fol. 12r; pl. XIX); in part historically, in
part symbolically, with the Virgin and John standing on one side of the Crucifix
and the psalmist receiving Christ's blood in a chalice and holding a paten with
hosts (fol. 67r; pl. CV).

[18] Stuttgart, Landesbibl., Cod. bibl. 4°, 2 fol. 9r. See Adolph Goldschmidt, *Die
deutsche Buchmalerei*, II (Florence-Munich, 1928), 20–21, 71, pl. 88.

strained gestures. The donor of the manuscript is allowed to kneel near Christ's feet, ready to embrace the cross.

In another Gospel manuscript the Crucifix is shown in all His loneliness in a rudimentary landscape (Figure 10).[19] His humility is emphasized by the fragility of His body. Whoever opened this Gospel book and looked at the miniature might have felt urged to contemplate calmly the past suffering of Christ.

An Anglo-Saxon miniature, on the other hand, combines expressive and symbolic elements.[20] Cramped into an angular posture, Christ hangs on the cross in the agony of death. He is smaller than Mary and John, and thus closer in size to the donor, who ardently embraces the cross. The cross itself is green, hewn from a living tree, its branches cut off, and refers to the tree of life. With an energetic gesture the Virgin reaches upwards to Christ's wound as if she were the Church, ready to receive Christ's blood in a chalice. The figure of John is equally unconventional. He draws away from Christ while looking back with great intensity and writing in a book as if under immediate inspiration.

Two miniatures of the Crucifixion painted about 980 by monks of the Reichenau School revert to a more historical kind of representation and even indicate two separate moments during the Crucifixion.

The first miniature shows some resemblance to the Crucifixion scene in the Rabula Gospels (Figures 11 and 4).[21] As in that manuscript Christ is fully clothed and crucified between the two thieves. At the foot of the cross the soldiers are gambling. Christ is still alive while Stephaton raises the stick with the sponge of vinegar. By their gestures Mary and John express their sorrow. In contrast to the Rabula Gospels the whole group is not set against a landscape, but silhouetted against a plain background with Christ dominating the scene by the larger cross and its golden color.

[19] Giessen, Universitätsbibl., Cod. 660, fol. 188r. See Goldschmidt, *Die deutsche Buchmalerei*, II, 20–21, 70.

[20] New York, Pierpont Morgan Libr., Ms. 709. See Hanns Swarzenski, *The Berthold Missal* (New York, 1943), fig. 1.

[21] Trier, Stadtbibl., Cod. 24, fol. 83v. See Hubert Schiel, *Codex Egberti der Stadtbibliothek Trier* (Basle, 1960), pp. 137ff.

In the following miniature Christ is already dead and Longinus pushes the spear into His side (Figure 12).[22] Here the cross is emphasized by its place on top of a mound.

A somewhat later miniature of the same school contains some components of the first Crucifixion scene in the Egbert Gospels, but there is an obvious change in formal and expressive aims and a greater stress on inherent symbolical possibilities.[23] The figures of the Virgin and John have become larger than those of the tormentors. Rather than expressing their grief, Mary and John point with symmetrical gestures toward Christ, thus stressing the importance of His self-sacrifice. Christ no longer hangs meekly on the cross, contained within its contours. His head rises above the horizontal cross-beam.

Still another miniature of a *Canticum Canticorum* Codex painted in the same workshop shows the Crucifix taken out of the historical context of the Crucifixion and made part and goal of an ideal procession of saints.[24] The procession begins in the center of the middleground with a scene of baptism by which the faithful are admitted into the church. Then the procession winds its way in a beautiful curve upwards to the crucified Christ. Next to Him a female figure holds a cross-staff and welcomes the first saint of the procession. She is the personification of the Church. Her presence near the cross can be explained by a passage in the Epistle to the Ephesians (5:25): "Christ also loved the Church and gave Himself for it."

Thus the representations of the Crucifixion around the year 1000 encompass the greatest possible span of formal and expressive possibilities. The miniatures can concentrate on Christ or show Him among various other figures, the Virgin and John, the two thieves, the soldiers and tormentors, the donors of the manuscripts, or an

---

[22] Fol. 84v. See Schiel, *Codex Egberti*, pp. 139–140.

[23] Bamberg, Staatl. Bibl., Ms. A II 42, fol. 68v. See Heinrich Wölfflin, *Die Bamberger Apokalypse*, 2nd ed. (Munich, 1921), pl. 54. This Crucifixion probably goes back to the type of representation exemplified by an eighth-century fresco in S. Maria Antiqua in Rome. See Thoby, *Le Crucifix des Origines au Concile de Trente*, pl. VIII.

[24] Bamberg, Staatl. Bibl., Ms. A I 47, fol. 4v. See Hanns Swarzenski, *Vorgotische Miniaturen*, 2nd ed. (Königstein i.T., 1931), p. 30.

ideal group of saints. These varying combinations are factors that determine in part the meaning of the Crucifix. Seen as a whole, the scenes may be lyrical or dramatic in character, narrative or symbolic in varying degrees. And it should be added that only a small number of examples could be discussed.

Once more we might look at the Crucifixion on the book-cover of the Morgan Library (Figure 1). We might realize again some characteristics which we have now observed in earlier representations: the importance of symbolic differentiation of size and the intention to give the upper part of Christ's figure greater strength than its lower part, so that only the lower part of His body is akin to the bodies of Mary and John.

We may realize again that the scene of Christ crucified is complemented by the representation of Christ in Majesty, one an earthly event, the other a heavenly vision. The representation of Christ in Majesty on this book-cover is determined by several factors: first, by His particular place in a mandorla, an ideal area of existence; second, by attending Angels proclaiming His glory; third, by His meaningful relation to the Crucifixion underneath.

I would like to discuss now a few examples of Christ in Majesty. They will show us how He may be accompanied either by Seraphim, as Isaiah saw the Lord in a vision, or by the four apocalyptic creatures surrounding the Son of man, as it was revealed to John according to the Book of Revelation. Additional figures or figure groups may either surround Christ or be subordinated to Him in order to enrich the meaning of Christ in Majesty.

One of the earliest examples of this type of representation is a panel from the wooden doors of S. Sabina in Rome, carved about 430 (Figure 13).[25] In the upper part of the relief Christ in Majesty appears to Peter, Paul, and Mary underneath. He stands among the Alpha and Omega within a circular wreath, a symbol of cosmic perfection and of an ideal space. In the four corners of the upper part the heads of the four apocalyptic creatures appear. According to the Book of Revelation they surround the throne of

[25] See E. H. Kantorowicz, "The King's Advent," *Art Bulletin*, XXVI (1944), 223ff.

the Lord. There is no throne in the relief and the Lord is standing. The relief is therefore not a literal representation of a specific passage in the Book of Revelation, but it has the apocalyptic connotations of the Second Coming of Christ at the end of time. The composition of the upper half of the relief is determined by its geometrical layout. A perfect circle contains Christ. The heads of the four creatures are so placed that Christ is equidistantly related to each member of the tetrad.

Two miniatures, both painted about the middle of the eighth century, one by the Irish monk who designed the Crucifixion in the St. Gall Gospels, the other by an artist of Merovingian France, vary in concept, although both glorify Christ. The Irish miniature shows Christ between two Angels above a group of smaller figures. The French miniature represents Christ in the midst of a circle related to a tetrad of figures in satellite circles.

In the St. Gall miniature the half-figure of Christ, completely flattened out into a decorative design, is prominent in the upper center.[26] He holds a small cross as a symbol of His victory over sin and death. He appears as the judge on the last day, attended by Angels blowing their trumpets. Underneath, the twelve Apostles, appointed by Christ to be His helpers in the Last Judgment, form a tight compositional pattern. By the sharp turn of their heads and the pattern of their hands pointing diagonally inwards and upwards they emphasize the power of Christ.

The French miniature in the Gundohinus Gospels shows the apocalyptic Christ, now enthroned and flanked by two Angels among the apocalyptic creatures which because of the books they are holding should be understood as the Symbols of the four Evangelists.[27]

One might say that the artist succeeded in stressing the head of Christ by a tremendous halo, and setting Christ's head off from His body by the clear horizontal formed by the upper edge of the throne's back. Yet at the same time the geometric framework of

[26] St. Gall, Stiftsbibl., Ms. 51, p. 267. Duft and Meyer, *Irish Miniatures*, p. 101, pl. XIV.

[27] Autun, Bibl. Munic., Ms. 3, fol. 12a. See Zimmermann, *Vorkarolingische Miniaturen*, pp. 182ff, pl. 80.

the composition based on the exact relation of a large central circle to smaller ones in the corners shows the shortcomings of this particular artist. The smaller circles are imperfectly drawn — as are the figures — and unevenly placed in relation to the central circle.

A Northumbrian miniature in the Codex Amiatinus of the late seventh century, on the other hand, apparently a close copy of a Mediterranean miniature, does not show any of these shortcomings of design or waverings in the composition (Figure 14).[28] Here the central group is enclosed by multiple concentric circles and fits harmoniously into the round shape. The peripheral figures are not enclosed in circles so that a further comparison with the French miniature may not seem justified. We should, however, observe that in the Northumbrian work two tetrads are represented, the four Evangelists and their Symbols. Although not related to Christ by the geometrical means of equidistant circles, they are arranged in a very meaningful way. The four Symbols are closer to the central axis formed by Christ. The Evangelists fill the corners. They turn inward like their Symbols and thereby accentuate the central axis, that is, Christ.

This more ambitious type of configuration was further developed and compositionally clarified in Carolingian art. At the same time, the figure of Christ was given a more specific meaning stemming from a controversy then rampant about the true substance of the Eucharist.

A miniature in a Bible illuminated for Charles the Bald about 845 shows Christ in the center, holding a small circular disc in His right hand (Figure 15).[29] Just at that time theologians debated the question whether it was the flesh of Christ who had once suffered death on the cross or the flesh of Christ in heaven, no longer suffering, which provides every day the substance for the Eucha-

[28] Florence, Bibl. Mediceo-Laurenziana, Cod. Amiat. I, fol. 769v. See F. Saxl, "The Ruthwell Cross," *England and the Mediterranean Tradition* (Oxford, 1945), pp. 16–17.

[29] Paris, Bibl. Nat., Ms. lat. 1, fol. 330v. See Wilhelm Koehler, *Die Karolingischen Miniaturen* I, *Die Schule von Tours*, Text, II (Berlin, 1933), pp. 132ff; Hans Bernh. Meyer, "Zur Symbolik frühmittelalterlicher Majestasbilder," *Das Münster*, XIV (1961), 73ff.

rist.[30] The miniature gives a visible answer to this question as it was officially adopted by the Church and backed by the emperor. It is Christ in Majesty, no longer suffering, who holds the host. Here Christ's figure is enclosed by a combination of two circles, the upper one denoting the absolute sphere of heaven. Christ sits on a still smaller circle denoting the firmament with its stars. The lowest section of this circle, still studded with stars, is singled out to serve as a footstool for Christ.

Closest to Christ are the Symbols of the Evangelists; they imply by their place that as sources of inspiration for the Evangelists they owe their power to Christ.

The corner medallions of the rhombus-like frame that surrounds Christ and the Symbols contain busts of the four major Prophets. In the corners of the page sit the four Evangelists, fulfilling their tasks under the inspiration of their Symbols.

The style of the figures, we should realize, is not abstracted to any great degree, compared with the figure style of the Merovingian age or Irish art. The Evangelists seem even to exist three-dimensionally in sections of three-dimensional space. It is the particular arrangement of the figures that expresses an idea, namely the idea of Christ's relation to the ones who predicted His coming and to the ones who recorded His work of salvation. An ingenious composition based on a framework of geometrical parts telescopes the essence of the two Testaments and clarifies their relation to Christ.

About twenty-five years later the same type of miniature was re-created for Charles the Bald in the Codex Aureus of St. Emmeram.[31] It is not, as one could have expected, an exact copy of the earlier miniature but rather a variation on the same theme. Christ is shown in the same attitude, but He is no longer enclosed by an ample eight-like combination of two circles but by a tighter oval mandorla. The medallions of the four Prophets are more closely related to Him because the four Symbols are now so placed

[30] See Koehler, *Die Karolingischen Miniaturen, loc. cit.*
[31] Munich, Bayer. Staatsbibl., Cod. lat. 1400, fol. 6v. See *Bayerns Kirche im Mittelalter* (Munich, 1960), pl. 11.

that they are nearer the Evangelists they inspire. Although close to each other, Evangelists and Symbols are separated by curved lines; yet this boundary is overcome by the intensity with which the Evangelists look at the sources of their inspiration. Throughout, the figures have grown in size in relation to the whole page. The effect is one of greater tension of the whole composition. Thus changes in style and expressive intensity occur even where an artist was asked to represent the same elements to be found in an earlier Bible commissioned by the same ruler.

In the Sacramentary of Charles the Bald Christ is again holding the host, but He is stressed in His majesty by different means (Figure 16).[32] Shown in the image of Isaiah's vision, He is related to both the angelic beings in heaven and the elements of the natural world. In the lower corners the personifications of Water with a jug and of Earth suckling children are represented. The natural atmospheric blue sky over water and earth differs from the unnatural green above signifying heaven.

When we considered the theme of the Crucifixion we saw how miniature painters of the tenth and eleventh centuries explored to the fullest possibilities inherent in earlier representations. The same could be said of the theme of Christ in Majesty. Two German miniatures must suffice to give us an idea of the wide scope of representations. They show Christ in the same posture and with the same gestures of blessing and holding the book. Yet significant variety is achieved by different configurations and by changes in the seat given to Christ.

In a miniature of a Gospel book from Cologne, to be dated in the first half of the eleventh century, Christ is related to the four major Prophets and the Symbols of the Evangelists, all of them acclaiming Christ (Figure 17).[33] As in the earlier miniature painted for Charles the Bald (Figure 15), Christ is enclosed by a two-circle combination, but instead of part of the firmament a small circle signifying the earth provides His footstool. According to

[32] Paris, Bibl. Nat., Ms. lat. 1141, fol. 6r.
[33] Bamberg, Staatl. Bibl., Ms. Bibl. 94, fol. 9v. See Goldschmidt, *Die deutsche Buchmalerei*, II, 21, 73.

Isaiah (66:1) the Lord says: "The heaven is my throne and the earth is my footstool." [34]

In another miniature of the same manuscript Christ, accompanied by two Seraphim, sits on an enormous cosmos that is carefully subdivided and inhabited by various figures and figure groups (Figure 18).[35] The sections sliced off at top and bottom contain in the upper parts the personifications of Fire and Air, holding the sun and the moon, in the lower parts Water with a fish and Earth with a child. The rest of the cosmos is separated horizontally into two parts, the upper one inhabited by Angels holding the footstool of Christ and worshipping Him. The lower part is given over to mankind represented by two scenes of baptism.

Thus even the illuminations of a single manuscript can make us aware of the variety with which Christ in Majesty was related to different types of figure compositions, a variety which determines the meaning.

In the miniature just discussed the total configuration has primarily a cosmological meaning. It shows Christ as the creator and ruler of the world with its four elements, its upper and lower regions, the realms of the Angels and of mankind. "Everything is made by Christ," says the inscription on the horizontal dividing band, "and without Christ nothing is made." [36] In the other miniature the total configuration has primarily a christological meaning. It shows Christ in relation to prediction and fulfillment of the two Testaments.

What main conclusions can we then draw from our observations? One might say that Early Christian art provided the ingredients for both more naturalistic and more abstract representa-

[34] In a somewhat earlier miniature Christ is shown in lonely splendor (Koblenz, Staatsarchiv, Cod. 701, fol. 127r; Goldschmidt, *Die deutsche Buchmalerei*, II, 6–7, 35, pl. 14a). Enclosed by a mandorla in the colors of the rainbow, He sits on a blue globe. His feet rest on the same kind of a small circle as in the miniature just discussed, but now the meaning that this is the earth has become obvious. Not only has the small circle a brownish color; there is also the suggestion of some rocks and flowers.

[35] Fol. 154v. See Goldschmidt, *Die deutsche Buchmalerei*, II, 21, 73.

[36] "Omnia per Christum facta sunt et sine Christo factum est nihil." See John I:3.

tions of Christ crucified and the ingredients for the image of Christ in Majesty.

Whenever representational art tended to be more abstract, be it in the Crucifixion panel of the S. Sabina doors or in Irish and Merovingian works, the theological idea of the two natures combined in the person of Christ could be immediately made visible. Whenever art tended to be less abstract, be it in the Early Christian ivory of the Crucifixion or in the Crucifixion miniatures of the Carolingian Renaissance and of later centuries, the idea of the two natures was not made visible in an obvious manner, while greater emphasis was placed on representing the various attitudes of Christ and of the holy witnesses of the Crucifixion.

Intricate ideographical schemata stressing Christ in Majesty were created in the Carolingian era and succeeding centuries not because of any abstractness of figure design but because of ingenious geometrical layouts of the composition.

) LYNN WHITE, JR. (

THE LIFE OF THE SILENT MAJORITY

FROM its beginnings until very recently, written history has been a history of the upper classes by the upper classes and for the upper classes. Literacy was the perquisite of small ruling groups. The human record normally has been confined to the interests and activities of those who recorded it, and its interpretation has been both constricted and tinctured by their values and concerns.

During the later eighteenth and the nineteenth centuries, North America and Western Europe established political democracies, and in the twentieth century the industrialized nations have gone far toward achieving an economic democracy which is rapidly abolishing the old functional division between aristocrats and commonality. Both political democracy and economic democracy have demanded not only universal literacy but also a rapidly rising general level of personal cultivation. Yet we are only now beginning to realize that the inherited substance of our culture, despite its vast riches, is in many ways inadequate to our own times because it was originally cast in an obsolete aristocratic mold. The novel task of our generation is to create a democratic culture to match our political and economic structures.

History is central to such an adventure. We must write — and write from scratch — the history of all mankind including the hith-

85

erto silent majority, and not merely that of the tiny vocal fraction which dominated the rest. Indeed, it is only in this larger context that we can really understand even the aristocrats; for just as a plowed field, by evaporation, brings subsoil minerals to the surface, so every aristocracy has fertilized itself by capillary action from the lower strata. While it is axiomatic that, within the limits of their means, these subordinate groups have aped the noblesse, it seems probable that, quite unconsciously, commoners who managed to percolate upward carried with them attitudes and habits of thinking which eventually reshaped aristocratic mores. Thus the increased social mobility of the later fourteenth century, following the Black Death, would seem to be related to the rapid changes in the higher culture of that period.

Because modern Western Europe and America emerged by almost imperceptible stages from the Middle Ages, medieval history has a high interest for the social and cultural genetics of the twentieth century. Moreover, in both regions the bulk of the population is descended biologically from the peasantry of the Middle Ages. It stands to reason that something of our mentality and emotions, as well as our chromosomes, is inherited from them. Can we discover this legacy?

The scholarly literature on peasant life seems to have neglected the earliest detailed description of medieval rustic households.[1] Shortly after 1050, in southern Germany, there was written *Ruodlieb*, a Latin versified novel. Although the author was presumably a cleric, his intention was simply to entertain. Ruodlieb, a young knight, leaves his mother in charge of his inherited lands and fares forth to a variety of adventures. After ten years he hears that his mother is getting old and lonely, so he starts toward home. As he is journeying he is joined by a rascally redhead. The road being muddy, the redhead starts riding through the adjacent fields and is promptly beaten by indignant peasants. As evening comes on, the two travelers approach a village. The redhead calls to a shepherd

[1] *Ruodlieb*, ed. E. H. Zeydel (Chapel Hill, N.C., 1959), V, 611, to VIII, 129, pp. 80–100.

asking for the names of prosperous persons who might put them up for the night. The shepherd replies that it would be a poor man indeed who could not take in two like them and stable their horses, and that there were many thereabout who would not be embarrassed if a count with a hundred retainers asked hospitality.

Having thus adequately insulted the horsemen, the shepherd goes on to suggest that they stay with a former widow who has a big house near the beginning of the village, and who had recently married the young manager of her properties. This is not to the redhead's liking: "Est vetus hic aliquis," he asks, "cui sit pulcherrima coniunx?" — "Isn't there some old man here with a pretty wife?" There is indeed, and the shepherd expresses no high opinion of the wench's morals.

Ruodlieb, our hero, who has more of the Tennysonian than of the medieval Galahad in his temperament, chooses the shepherd's first recommendation and spends a most comfortable night. The redhead, needless to say, goes to the house of the old man with the flirtatious wife, seduces her, is discovered, and murders the husband. Next morning he is tried in the village church before a judge assisted by what appears to be a jury, and is executed.

The author of the poem has no sociological intent: his description of German peasant life in the middle of the eleventh century is the more valuable because he is simply telling a picaresque story in a context familiar to his audience. Here we view a lively, self-confident, prosperous agrarian society. The village is of considerable size. The houses are built around courts which include stables, barns, storehouses, and latrines. There are many cattle, horses, sheep, goats, hogs, chickens, geese, and bees, not to mention pet dogs and cats, and a large establishment has several hired servants. There is plenty of food, including meat, and for special occasions one drinks wine or mead. Surplus production is sold for money, and there is some participation in commerce: spices are twice mentioned, and the hussy has a fur robe. At the house where Ruodlieb stays, a cup magnificently carved of walnut wood, and ornamented with gold, is brought out in his honor. Our author, however, is not romanticizing the peasant: the older men in particular are unkempt, dirty, and rough in their manners.

What are we to think of the fact that this eleventh-century picture of northern peasant life is considerably happier than those found in such well-known poems as *Meir Helmbrecht*, two hundred years later, and *Piers Plowman* in the fourteenth century? The key to the difference is the fact that these works have a moralizing intent: they are denunciations of abuses which undoubtedly existed, but this circumstance should warn us not to consider their descriptions normative. *Ruodlieb* may be trusted as more objective because it has as little purpose of arousing compassion for the peasant as of making us envious of him: the author is merely spinning a good yarn in the setting of the society which he knows.

We have reason to believe that the prosperity of the northern European peasantry which is mirrored in *Ruodlieb* was a relatively recent achievement, and that when the poem was written rural life was in rapid flux. Between 1060 and 1088 a perceptive monk of Saint-Père at Chartres compiled the cartulary of his abbey, which contained no documents earlier than the late ninth century. In his Preface he remarks, "I must warn the reader that the first documents which I shall transcribe will be seen to differ greatly from present usage; for the documents written long ago and now found in our archive show that the rustics of that period did not in any way observe the customs regarding services to which the modern peasants of our own time hold, nor do we today use the words for things which were then part of the common speech." [2]

The problem of measuring the pace of change in Europe's rural life is the more difficult because, so far as I know, we have no glimpse of a rustic establishment earlier than *Ruodlieb* except that in the anonymous *Moretum*, a poem stylistically so charming that from the tenth century onward it was often ascribed to Virgil. Its date has been much disputed, but a *terminus post quem* can be set by archaeology, since it mentions a form of quern which has not been securely established as existing earlier than the fourth or

[2] *Cartulaire de l'abbaye de Saint-Père de Chartres*, ed. B. E. C. Guérard (Paris, 1840), I, 14.

fifth century.[3] The pattern of peasant life seen in *Moretum* is amazingly primitive — almost neolithic. The evidence is the more valuable because the poet's intention, as in *Ruodlieb*, is descriptive rather than moralistic. But since *Moretum's* scene is Italy, and the contrast between the Mediterranean and the transalpine climates would normally dictate differences in the styles of agriculture, we cannot judge whether the condition of the northern peasantry was better or worse than that in Italy when *Moretum* was written. One suspects that it was equally stark.

The peasantry which are revealed about 1050 in *Ruodlieb*, then, are a new social phenomenon of great significance for our understanding not only of the later Middle Ages but also of the origins of the modern world. What do we know of their emergence?

Even to tillers of the soil, not all of life is work. Yet, much of it is labor of the hardest sort, and anything which changes the pattern of that labor, or improves the yield from it, alters the entire tone of life. We have begun to see that rural life has never been static, and that in certain periods it has changed with great rapidity. Evidence has been accumulating recently to show that in northern Europe, from the sixth century to the end of the ninth, a series of innovations occurred which consolidated to form a remarkably efficient new way of exploiting the soil.[4] It saved human labor and notably increased the peasant's productivity. By the eleventh century, its full effects were being felt. It is this agricultural revolution which accounts for the prosperity of the peasants in *Ruodlieb*.

What, specifically, were these changes in agricultural methods? The distinctive implement of medieval agriculture in the North was the *carruca*, a heavy plow, usually with wheels, capable of

[3] *Appendix Vergiliana*, ed. O. Ribbeck (Leipzig, 1868), 138, line 126; for the dating, cf. L. T. White, *Medieval Technology and Social Change* (Oxford, 1962), p. 109.

[4] For details see White, *Medieval Technology and Social Change*, pp. 39–78. The admirable work of G. Duby, *L'économie rurale et la vie des campagnes dans l'occident médiéval*, 2 vols. (Paris, 1962), commences with the ninth century. Nevertheless, Duby, I, 75, accepts as valid the evidence that the heavy plow was known to the Slavs "entre le V⁰ et le X⁰ siècle."

turning over a furrow rather than merely scratching the soil as the Mediterranean plows did. It was not known in the Rhineland in the first decade of the sixth century when *Lex Salica* was still using *carruca* to mean a two-wheeled cart. There are linguistic indications that some Slavic groups were employing such a plow by 568. By 643 it is found in the Po Valley, and by the 720's *Lex Alemannorum* shows that in southwestern Germany the word *carruca* now meant the new wheeled plow.[5] Presumably it reached Scandinavia about the same time, whence it was taken to Britain by the Norse invasions of the late ninth century.

The first great advantage of the new plow was that it could handle heavy alluvial soils which gave better crops than the lighter soils suited to the older scratch-plow. Second, since its moldboard turned over the furrow, cross-plowing was unnecessary, and this saved human labor. Third, it became possible to plow fields shaped in long strips with the earth gradually mounding toward the center of the strip because the moldboard normally turned the furrow inward toward the center of the strip. This arrangement greatly assisted field drainage, an important matter in the wet northern climate. Obviously, if peasants could manage to adopt the new plow, it was much to their advantage.

There were obstacles, however. Colter, horizontal share, and moldboard offered far more resistance to the soil than the old plow. Whereas a scratch-plow generally could be pulled by a yoke of two oxen, the new plow often required eight oxen. No peasant owned so many. The only solution was a pooling of the oxen of several peasants to form a cooperative plow-team, and a division of plowed strips according to the contribution of each. Such a pooling, however, would be impractical in sparsely settled areas, or in hamlets so small that the plan would collapse if one or two

[5] Duby, *L'économie rurale*, I, 76, believes that in this passage (xcvi, §2, in *Monumenta Germaniae Historica*, Leges, III, 80, 116: "si carrucam inviolat, aut rumpit rotas primerias"; another text reads ". . . rotas de davante") the *Lex Alemannorum* preserves the earlier meaning of "cart" for *carruca*. But a two-wheeled cart has no *front* wheels; and would breaking the *rear* wheels of a four-wheeled cart bring no penalty? The law clearly refers to an instrument equipped with wheels *in front*, that is, to the heavy plow.

oxen died or were stolen. Thus, while the increased productivity of the new technique would eventually increase population, a certain density of settlement was required for its introduction.

Yet the existence of an established peasant population was itself an obstacle to the spread of the new plow: the fields cultivated by the old type of plow had to be cross-plowed and therefore tended to be squarish in shape; the laying out of the strips which were the most efficient shape of field for the new plow would require destruction of all existing field-marks and individual property rights. This would be psychologically so difficult that we can safely assume that the new agricultural system spread primarily through reclamation and the settlement of lands hitherto uncultivated.

It would seem, in fact, that after a long period of decline culminating in the fearful plagues of the sixth century, Europe's population began to swing upward again, and with increasing momentum.[6] From the seventh century onward, there is indication of the clearing of forests and the increase of cultivation, presumably much of it in the pattern of the new agricultural system with its higher productivity.

The novel shaping of fields in strips involved unprecedented methods of agricultural cooperation. Squarish fields could be efficiently fenced or hedged to protect growing crops; strip fields could not. The new plow therefore required that all the arable land of a peasant community be divided into two roughly equal parts,

[6] There can be no statistical certainty in this matter: scholars working with considerable masses of archaeological material, especially burials, arrive at rough judgments of relative densities of population at different periods. É. Salin, *La Civilisation mérovingienne*, IV (Paris, 1959), 451, believes that the low point in Europe was reached about 500 A.D. Epidemics, however, were so widespread and repeated between 542 and 590 that recovery in the sixth century seems improbable, and Salin does not offer tangible evidence of it. In recent years certain archaeologists (cf. White, *Medieval Technology and Social Change*, p. 54, n. 1) have concluded that, in central and southern Germany and the Rhineland at least, repopulation began at the end of the sixth century, accompanied by colonization and reclamation of new lands, and this dating is preferred by J. C. Russell, "Late Ancient and Medieval Population," *Transactions of the American Philosophical Society*, XLVIII, iii (1958), 42, 140. Doubtless the revival was not simultaneous in all parts of Europe. The exact definition of its geographic and temporal variations is a matter of importance, since the nadir of population marks one of the few defensible frontiers between antiquity and the Middle Ages.

one to be planted in the autumn and the other left fallow to regain its fertility for the next year's planting. Each of these two big fields was fenced against animals, but there were no barriers between the strips within each big field, which therefore was called an "open field."

There were unexpected practical advantages of this open-field arrangement. In the earlier period, cattle and sheep of a village seem generally to have been led to forage in the forest or on wild pasture where their manure was lost. Now, under the two-field system, they were habitually put into the fallow field and then onto the stubble of the year's arable after the harvest was gathered. Thus the bringing of new land under cultivation certainly did not reduce the production of meat, dairy products, hides, and wool, but probably increased it. Moreover, droppings of the animals on the open fields notably improved the yield of cultivated crops. Thus the herding economy of the Germans and the cereal agriculture of the Mediterranean were integrated into a new and more rewarding pattern.

In the later eighth century there was another advance, beginning, it would appear, in the region between the Seine and the Rhine. There is some evidence that, in contrast to the autumn planting of southern lands, the earliest agriculture of the Baltic area employed a spring planting. In Charlemagne's reign we find some peasants operating not with two open fields but with three: a fallow, an autumn planting primarily of wheat, barley, or rye, and a spring planting largely of oats and legumes. This three-field rotation of crops put greater demands on the soil than the two-field rotation, but the extensive use, in the spring planting, of legumes with their nitrogen-fixing properties maintained fertility adequately.

For intricate reasons of internal economy, a shift from the two- to three-field system enabled a peasant community to increase its production by 50 per cent, provided that they could clear enough new land. The result was a tremendous spurt in reclamation. Even where adequate new land was not available, or where it was too marginal to sustain the more intensive rotation, the northern peasants generally did what they could to get the benefits of the new system: when they were unable to reclaim a third field from the wild or found it unfeasible to redistribute the arable of their village among three rather than two fields, they nevertheless divided the planted field into two parts, sowing one in the autumn and the other in the spring. The scholarly discussion of field systems has frequently been clouded by failure to recognize that in northern Europe even two-field villages normally planted in the spring as well as in the autumn and thus in some measure enjoyed the benefits of the triennial rotation.

It is fundamental for an understanding of Europe's history that the spring planting was possible only north of the Loire and the Alps, because to the south of that line (except for pockets in northern Spain, Provence, and the Po Valley) summer rains were insufficient. As Henri Pirenne accurately observed, in the eighth century the focus of Europe shifted from the shores of the Mediterranean to the great plains around the Channel and the North Sea where it has remained ever since. The essential reason is to be found in the new productivity of the northern peasantry.

In Charlemagne's last years we find the first evidence of still another innovation which eventually added much to the prosperity of northern agriculture, as distinct from that of the Mediterranean: the modern horse harness. Yokes were well suited to the anatomy of oxen, but were singularly inefficient for horses or mules. The modern horse harness, consisting of a rigid collar attached to the load by lateral traces or shafts, may have come out of central Asia, but it first appears in Europe in a Carolingian illumination of about the year 800. With the new harness, which cost no more than the old, a horse could pull four or five times the load which he could handle with a yoke. For the first time horses were available for plowing, harrowing, and heavy hauling. Moreover, there was great advantage in using them, since they are much swifter than oxen and save human time.

There were, nevertheless, difficulties in the way. Especially in a moist climate, the hooves of a horse are much more vulnerable than those of an ox, and heavy labor quickly breaks them or wears them down. The invention of the nailed horseshoe has long been a matter of ardent controversy, and has been claimed not only for the Romans but even for the pre-Roman Celts. Fortunately archaeologists are coming to realize that the stratification of horseshoes is a matter for great caution. When a horse bogs in mud, the suction caused by its efforts to pull its feet up may well deposit a shoe two or three feet below the surface, and invariably, it would seem, adjacent to a fragment of Aretine pottery. When a horse loses a shoe in a rodent's hole, the small inhabitant of the burrow pulls it downward as often as outward; and there, below, is sure to be a coin of Vespasian. Even earthworms complicate the problem. Where there is a heavy population of worms, they may deposit as much as a quarter of an inch of droppings annually on the surface, with the result that small heavy objects like horseshoes work down into the soil. Since there is no literary or iconographic evidence of horseshoes in antiquity, one is driven for assurance to burials of horses with their masters. The earliest unambiguous archaeological indication of nailed horseshoes comes from rider-graves of the Yenesei basin in Siberia dating from the transition between the ninth and tenth centuries. Simultaneously, they are mentioned in a Byzantine text and in a Latin poem written in Germany. Is it merely a coincidence that at that same moment, from Norway, we have the first word of horses being used routinely for plowing? Surely horseshoes as well as the modern harness were prerequisites.

As more scholars become aware of problems of this sort, more evidence will turn up. It is worth noting that nailed horseshoes were habitual, at least for ridden horses, in *Ruodlieb* (V, 602). Although the British Isles seem to have lagged somewhat, by the end of the eleventh century horses were displacing oxen in agriculture, or had already done so, in regions as separated as northern France and Kievan Russia. Not, however, in the Mediterranean lands which climatically were confined to the autumn planting. In the region of summer rains the spring planting provided an abundance of oats which enabled the northern peasants, save on marginal soils, to use the more costly horse in place of the cheaper ox. The ox, however, was expensive of human time and spirit, and the southern peasants plodded behind him because they could do nothing else. The agricultural revolution of the northern Middle Ages which makes intelligible the peasant life pictured in *Ruodlieb* is relevant not only to Europe's economic life but also to its psychic development.

Agrarian archaeology has begun to inform us that as early as the eleventh century the peasants of the North were beginning to regroup their dwellings. The ox is so slow that plowmen using it had to live fairly close to their fields. When the faster horse came into use for rural labor, one could efficiently live much farther from the fields. The mathematical rule relating the length of a radius to the area of a circle came into play. Many tiny hamlets were abandoned; the peasants agglomerated into the sort of big village which we see in *Ruodlieb*: its economic base is strictly agricultural, but it has tinges of urbanism. In such a village of two or three hundred families one could enjoy not only better defense but also a fine big church, the prompter ministrations of a priest in moments of crisis, more company, better gossip, and more frequent contact with merchants and their wares. In 1939 a German scholar bewailed the "spiritual urbanization" of the peasantry of the thirteenth century.[7] We are coming to see, however, that by the thirteenth century the process was already at least two hundred years old and that its presupposition was the substitution of horse for ox in farm labor.

The availability of horses for heavy hauling likewise much expanded the horizons of the northern peasants. In the early fourteenth century Pegolotti says that wagons of goods drawn by horses travel more than twice as far in a day as those drawn by

[7] B. Huppertz, *Räume und Schichten bäuerlicher Kulturformen in Deutschland* (Bonn, 1939), pp. 134–137.

oxen.[8] The horse therefore greatly increased the range of markets in which a peasant might dispose of his surplus production, provided he had an adequate wagon.

The history of land transport before the railroad has scarcely been investigated. The pivoted front axle for wagons was known to the Romans and continued in use; but horses, with their swift and abrupt motions, could not safely be attached to a heavy load until the whipple-tree was invented. If traces connect a horse directly to the wagon, plow, or harrow, a left turn puts all the strain on the right trace, and vice versa, with danger of breaking the harness. However, if the traces are attached to the ends of a whipple-tree which in turn is linked at its center to the middle of the front of the load, the tug on the traces is equalized, the efficiency of pulling is maintained, and danger to the harness is eliminated. The whipple-tree therefore is essential to the full development of horse traction. I have not been able to find specific evidence of the whipple-tree earlier than the mule-drawn plow and the horse-drawn harrow in the border of the Bayeux Tapestry,[9] now generally dated not later than 1077. Since harrowing a field of heavy clods is such jolting work that a whipple-tree would be particularly useful, it is worth noting that the earliest reference to a horse harrowing is found in *Ruodlieb* (V, 468–469) a quarter century earlier. Moreover, the poet considers horse-harrowing quite customary. I therefore suspect that the whipple-tree, a grubby but important innovation in transportation, was produced by the sort of vigorous eleventh-century peasants whom we find in *Ruodlieb*.

The increased geographical range of habitual contacts made possible by the horse clearly affected the tone and tempo of peasant life. The spread of the watermill was equally significant. Water-powered grain mills, both the simple vertical-axle variety and the more complex geared kind which Vitruvius describes, first appear in the first century before Christ. Nevertheless, for

[8] F. Balducci Pegolotti, *La Pratica della Mercatura*, ed. A. Evans (Cambridge, Mass., 1936), p. 21.

[9] *The Bayeux Tapestry*, ed. F. Stenton (London and New York, 1957), pl. 12.

reasons which remain obscure, they did not become common until after the western Roman Empire disintegrated. Thereafter they keep turning up with increasing frequency all over Europe until by the year 1000 they are part of every rural landscape. Domesday Book of 1086 lists 5,624 mills for some 3,000 communities in England, and there are reasons to think that this count of mills is too low.[10] While we have no comparable statistical survey from the Continent, England was probably not technically in advance of the mainland. Many mills had gearing, and the millwright who built and repaired mills was a common figure among the villagers: together with the blacksmith he familiarized the peasantry with an advancing metallurgical and mechanical technology. In appraising the destiny of the Occident, one cannot exaggerate the importance of the fact that by the eleventh century in Europe — and, it would seem, in Europe alone — every peasant was living daily in the presence of at least one fairly complex, semiautomatic power machine. It is no accident that in the eleventh century water power is first applied to industrial processes other than milling: trip-hammer devices are found both in the forges of smiths and in watermills employed in the fulling of cloth fresh from the loom.[11] Our present labor-saving power technology is rooted in a peasant society which had already learned how to apply new implements, new animal power, and new management systems to the more efficient exploitation of the soil. The agricultural revolution of the early Middle Ages is the backdrop of the eleventh-century beginnings of the modern industrial revolution which has grown exponentially for the past nine hundred years.

Viewed in this perspective, the eleventh century marks a moment of primary mutation in the forms of human life. Is it possible to understand the mental and even emotional changes which enabled the silent masses of Europe's common people to achieve such a breakthrough?

[10] M. T. Hodgen, "Domesday Water Mills," *Antiquity*, XIII (1939), 266; R. Lennard, *Rural England, 1086–1135* (Oxford, 1959), pp. 278–280.

[11] B. Gille in *Histoire générale des techniques*, ed. M. Daumas (Paris, 1962), I, 467–468; White, *Medieval Technology and Social Change*, pp. 83–84.

We are beginning to see that the early Middle Ages in Europe witnessed a profound alteration of attitudes toward nature. This shift in the world view was based partly on the agricultural revolution of that era and partly on the revolution in popular religion which was occurring simultaneously.

In the days of the scratch-plow and squarish fields, land was distributed in units which were thought to be sufficient for the support of one family. The peasant paid rent, which was in effect taxes, to the owning-ruling aristocracy, but the assumption was subsistence farming — man was part of nature. The new heavy plow of northern Europe changed this. Since it demanded a cooperative plow-team, the strips which it plowed were distributed in proportion to a peasant's contribution to the team. Thus the standard of land distribution ceased to be the needs of a family and became the ability of a power engine to till the soil. No more fundamental modification in a man's relation to his environment can be imagined: he ceased to be nature's child and became her exploiter. We, who are descended from the peasants who first built such plows, inherit from them that aggressive attitude toward nature which is an essential element in modern culture. We feel so free to use nature for our purposes because we feel abstracted from nature and its processes.

This disinvolvement of man from nature was aided by the slow Christianization of the common people which occurred during the early Middle Ages. Christianity was at first a religion of cities, which embraced only a very small part of the population: as late as the end of the fifth century, at least in the West, there are indications that most peasants were still *pagani*. Even when there was external conformity with the new faith, the essence of popular religion long remained little affected. Merovingian archaeology reveals horrifyingly primitive religious attitudes.[12]

---

[12] Salin, *La Civilisation mérovingienne*, IV: *Les croyances* demonstrates in detail, *passim*, that the barbarian concept of religion as intensely practical, a device for manipulating ambient powers to secure peace of mind and physical well-being, was incorporated entire into Frankish Christianity. The warrior's marvelously laminated sword was designed to deal with visible foes, but the patterns on his sword-belt were equally directed toward fending off the invisible. Even traces of

Scholars have not yet examined in adequate detail one of the most significant chapters in European history: the gradual spread of the parish system out of the tiny cities into the rude countryside.[13] Not until church towers rose above cultivated fields did the new religion begin to modify the minds and emotions of most men.

Popular religion in antiquity was animistic. Every stream, every tree, every mountain contained a guardian spirit who had to be carefully propitiated before one put a mill in the stream, or cut the tree, or mined the mountain. While one could communicate with these myriad spirits, they were in no sense human: the half-bestial satyrs, centaurs, and mermaids were the symbols of their ambiguity. The Christian saint who displaced the *genius loci* as the most accessible spiritual entity in the new religion was very different. Although he might have favorite shrines, his ear was omnipresent. Moreover, he was completely a man, and could be approached in terms of human interests. The cult of saints ousted spirits from the material objects of nature and liberated mankind psychologically to exploit physical nature freely. The localized *daemon* of antiquity became the medieval demon, a malevolent fallen angel who shared the saint's abstraction from matter and place. One may regard the popular religion of the Middle Ages as gross superstition and still recognize that, as compared with its equivalent in antiquity, it was vastly more sophisticated, and that its new abstraction of spirit from matter fostered a new flexibility in the human utilization of matter.

In the new parish churches of the villages of the early Middle Ages the peasants knelt to talk to the saints. But in those same churches, very privately, they gradually learned to kneel also at

human sacrifice are found as late as the eighth century among nominally Christian populations. See p. 12.

[13] It would appear that rural churches began to be established in Italy in the later fifth century and north of the Alps in the sixth, but that the network of parishes was not complete, even in areas of old settlement, until the tenth century. There is no survey of the total movement and of its implications. Excellent regional sketches are C. E. Boyd, *Tithes and Parishes in Medieval Italy* (Ithaca, N.Y., 1952), pp. 47–74, and J. Godfrey, *The Church in Anglo-Saxon England* (Cambridge, Eng., 1962), pp. 310–330, 502–503.

the feet of the priest to confess their sins. This was a custom which seems to have been unknown to the Church in antiquity, when public confession and penance were practiced. So far as we can now see, private confession was an Irish innovation spread over Europe by Celtic missionaries in the later Merovingian and Carolingian periods. Under Irish influence, priests in northern Europe particularly came to be equipped with *Penitentials*, manuals for the examination of sin. They trained their illiterate parishioners in moral self-examination, spiritual introspection. In ancient paganism, popular religion had been largely public and corporate, little involved in concepts of personal ethics. The penitential discipline developed by the early medieval Church, and carried by the new network of parishes into the most remote regions of Europe, gradually led to profound changes in the spiritual conformation of peasant culture. It opened the experience of the common people to a new kind of highly personal, interiorized, religion. It confirmed the abstraction of spirit from all externals and thus enabled our European ancestors to cope the more freely with externals. The life of the silent masses during the early Middle Ages therefore marks a major stage in our effort to master both the impulses within us and the forces and resources external to us.

} JOHN C. MCGALLIARD {

BEOWULF AND BEDE

SINCE it became available to modern readers in the first edition, in 1815, the poem *Beowulf* has meant many different things to many men. It has been called a "folk" epic or a "natural" epic. Its plot has been labeled a nature myth. Some at one time considered it a patchwork of ballads or heroic lays. Others have regarded it as a heathen poem to which later interpolations have added a Christian "coloring." Formerly many of its admirers were embarrassed by what was deemed a plot unworthy of great art and a lack of narrative unity. It tells of a princely hero who in his youth slew two man-devouring monsters and in his old age, after a long reign as king, slew and was slain by a dragon. This folktale plot is conducted against a rich background of Germanic legends and historical traditions.

Critical study in recent decades has effectively established the poem as a work of high and careful art. As to structure, it balances the heroism of youth and age, with the transience of man's life as a unifying theme. Its numerous "digressions" are recognized as enhancing one or another aspect of a coherent work. We see that the hero's exploits are invested with ethical significance and thus with commensurate dignity. The poet's Christian point of view is recognized as basic and organic. Although in some sense it is the product of an oral tradition of poetry — like the *Iliad* and *Odyssey* — the language and diction are the achievement of a gifted artist.

Much remains unknown. The name and identity of the composer are lost; but he must have lived in England at some period between the late seventh and the early ninth centuries. Containing 3,182 alliterating lines, it is the longest extant poem in Old English — or Anglo-Saxon — and the only long poem dealing with Germanic traditional stories. It has acquired an enormous bibliography in the past hundred and fifty years. During the past century much effort has been spent in relating the quasi-historical incidents, episodes, and allusions in the poem to the over-all pattern of Germanic legend and tradition. Alliances and wars among Danes, Geats, Swedes, "Frisians," and other tribal nations have been traced with considerable success. The rise and decline of heroes and dynasties have been plausibly plotted. If, as Alcuin insisted, Ingeld has nothing to do with Christ, he has a great deal to do with the poetry of northern Europe. And it is likely enough that his story had a basis in history. Now, investigation of matters like these may throw light on the subjects treated or alluded to in *Beowulf*. It may enhance our knowledge of the *contents* of a poetic tradition inherited by the peoples of Anglo-Saxon England. But it can tell us little directly about the lives, the experiences, or the attitudes of the people after they had been settled in the new country for a century or two. For the events and allusions found in the poem have nothing to do with either the authentic or the fabulous history of *England*. Evidently people liked these stories of their Continental past. Otherwise they would not have been handed down. They would not have been available for the anonymous poet to weave into the carefully wrought fabric of his design. But what did the men and women of, say, eighth-century England really think of these tales of heroes and heroines who triumphed and suffered in fourth-, fifth-, or early sixth-century Scandinavia and adjacent areas? How remote or how close did their motives, deeds, and destinies seem to the poet and his contemporaries? How well could they be understood? Were the conditions and circumstances and human attitudes like or unlike?

For a number of years I have read and reread not only *Beowulf* but also the *Ecclesiastical History of the English People* by St. Bede, longer known as the Venerable Bede. This great work was written — or completed — in the year 731. I have been increasingly impressed by certain similarities or parallels between the poem and the history. Of course, there are no identical events. Bede deals with insular history, Romano-Celtic and English. The narrative of *Beowulf* never touches England at all. I need not elaborate the vast difference in kind which separates the two works. I have no reason to suspect an influence in either direction. Perhaps it should be added that I eschew and should deplore any effort to read the poem as political allegory. My approach is quite different. I propose to look at the two texts as complementary records of a common culture. I hope to demonstrate that they often supplement or corroborate or substantiate — and thus for us, the modern readers, *illuminate* — each other. And perhaps we shall see a little more clearly the relation of the poem, at least, to the age that produced it.

A pervasive topic in *Beowulf* and Bede alike is the struggle for power in one or another Scandinavian or Anglo-Saxon kingdom. Internal in origin, this might frequently involve other kingdoms as well if, as often happened, the loser took refuge at the court of another king. We may begin with Edwin of Northumbria, apt to be remembered by the modern reader of Bede's *History* because of the dramatic scenes accompanying his conversion to Christianity in the year 627.

Now Edwin had spent long years as a prince in exile because of the enmity of his predecessor, King Æthelfrith. Finally he was granted refuge by Rædwald, king of East Anglia. Æthelfrith's emissaries come to Rædwald, not once but twice, and urge him either to yield up Edwin or dispatch him on his own initiative. Rædwald, already persuaded, is recalled to right and obligation by his queen. Thus guided, he collects an army, defeats and slays Æthelfrith on the Mercian border, and enables Edwin to establish himself as king in Northumbria (616 or 617 A.D. — *Historia Ecclesiastica* 2.12).

If we turn now to *Beowulf*, we find parallels in an episode of the long and involved relationships between the Geats and the Swedes. After the redoubtable old Swedish king Ongentheow was slain in war with the Geats, his son Ohthere apparently succeeded him as king. But, upon Ohthere's death, his brother Onela seized power. Ohthere's sons, Eanmund and Eadgils, as either voluntary or involuntary exiles, sought refuge at the court of Heardred, king of the Geats. When Heardred received them hospitably, the Swedish ruler, Onela — more precipitate, it would seem, than Bede's Northumbrian Æthelfrith — invaded the country of the Geats. And Heardred was killed in the ensuing war. Here is the poet's account of these events.

"As wretched exiles, the sons of Ohthere came to him [that is, Heardred] over the sea . . ."

> Hyne wræcmæcgas
> ofer sæ sohtan,   suna Ohteres . . .   (2379–81)

". . . they had repudiated the ruler of the Scylfings, that is, the Swedes, that best of the sea-kings of those who distributed treasure in the realm of the Swedes, a well-known prince. For him [that is, Heardred] this was the end; there he, the son of Hygelac, got for his hospitality a death wound by the strokes of a sword . . ."

> Him þæt to mearce wearð;
> he þær [f]or feorme   feorhwunde hleat,
> sweordes swengum,   sunu Hygelaces . . .   (2384–86)

The victorious Onela now returned to his own land and Beowulf, the hero of the poem, succeeded his dead cousin Heardred as king of the Geats.

But there was a sequel, doubtless some years later. Eanmund was apparently killed in the engagement just recounted; but his brother Eadgils survived and prosecuted his claim to the Swedish throne. The poet tells how Beowulf helped him win success. "He [Beowulf] remembered a recompense of that slaughter in later days, became a friend to the destitute Eadgils; he assisted the son of Ohthere [Eadgils] with a company, with soldiers, and weapons; he [Eadgils] took vengeance for his chilling travels as an exile, he deprived the king [Onela] of his life" — and, of course, took his place as ruler of the Swedes.

> Se ðæs leodhryres   lean gemunde
> uferan dogrum,   Eadgilse wearð
> feasceaftum freond;   folce gestepte
> ofer sæ side   sunu Ohteres,
> wigum ond wæpnum;   he gewræc syððan
> cealdum cearsiðum,   cyning ealdre bineat.   (2391–96)

Now let us return to Bede for a few more reversals which may be rapidly reviewed. During King Edwin's reign in Northumbria, the historian tells us, the sons of the former king Æthelfrith "were banished, with a great number of young nobles, and so lived among the Scots and Picts." (*H. E.* 3.1.) After Edwin was killed in war against his great enemy Penda, the heathen king of Mercia, these princes returned home. The eldest, Eanfrid, became ruler of the northern part of Northumbria, known as Bernicia. Meanwhile, Edwin's widow and former queen, Ethelberga, returned with her young family to her native land of Kent. A little later, "for fear of the kings Eadbald and Oswald" — who after various disturbances had come to power in Northumbria — "she sent her two children into Gaul to be brought up in the court of King Dagobert, who was her friend [and cousin], and there they both died in their infancy . . ." (*H. E.* 2.20.) Our third item in this present series concerns the royal succession in Kent near the end of the seventh century, a time marking the boyhood of Bede and, incidentally, about the earliest feasible period for the composition of the poem *Beowulf*. (I speak of possibility; the probability is that it came rather later.) Bede's narrative is concise, and we may take it as it stands. "And in the same year, which is the 685th of the Lord's incarnation, died Hlothere king of Kent the 6th day of February, when he had himself reigned 12 years after his brother Egbert, who had reigned 9 years. For he [that is, Hlothere] was wounded in the battle of the South Saxons whom *Edric the son of Egbert* had gathered against him, and while he was yet in curing he died. And after him the said Edric reigned one year and a half: and after his death that kingdom was for some space of time brought to ruin through kings of uncertain right or not of the royal kin; until *the lawful king Wictred, that is to say, the son of Egbert,* was established on the throne, and by religion as well as by diligence delivered his people from foreign assault." (*H. E.* 4.26; translation of Thomas Stapleton, 1565; italics mine.)

We can hardly fail to observe that very often the pivot of strife is a contest between uncle (father's brother) and nephew. This is equally notable in Bede and in *Beowulf*. We have already noticed the struggle within the Swedish royal family. Now let us turn to the poet's treatment of Hrothgar, king of the Danes. Despite the ravages of the monster Grendel, from which the hero Beowulf comes as a deliverer, the Danish court is stately and splendid. Around the venerable, aged king are grouped his gracious queen Wealhtheow, his two (strangely) young sons, Hrethric and Hrothmund — and his nephew Hrothulf, son of his dead brother Halga. The poet couples uncle and nephew in the same half-line: "Hroð-gar and Hroþulf" (1017); he assures us that these "kinsmen" (*magas*, 1015) in that high hall were resolute and valiant (swiþ-hicgende/on sele þam hean, 1016); he even adds that Heorot (the name of the hall) was filled with friends (1017–18). And then, in just a line and a half, he slips in a premonition: the Danish nation was not involved in treachery *so far*:

> nalles facenstafas
> þeod-Scyldingas   þenden fremedon.   (1018–19)

The alliterative stress falls on the adverb *þenden*, "so far."

This is the beginning of a long and festive scene; the court is celebrating Beowulf's conquest of Grendel; gifts are presented to the hero; stories are told of past Danish glory; speeches are made. In one of these the queen, Wealhtheow, after congratulating Beowulf, adds these remarks: "I know my gracious Hrothulf, (know) that he will treat the young people kindly, if you, lord of the Scyldings [that is, Hrothgar, king of the Danes] leave the world before him; I expect that he will repay our sons with goodness — if he remembers all the favors and kindnesses that we two [herself and Hrothgar] did for his advantage and honor when he was still a boy." Then, according to the poem, she went and sat beside her sons, Hrethric and Hrothmund, in the part of the hall where the young people sat, along with Beowulf. A few moments later she presents a famous necklace to the hero; this calls for another speech. Within its sixteen lines, she makes two pleas on behalf of her children. She asks Beowulf to "be friendly in his counsel to these boys" (1219–20) and again to be "kind in deeds to my son." (1219–20 and 1226–27.) Then she concludes with this profession of confidence: "Here every warrior is true to the other, gentle in mood, loyal to his lord; thanes are trustworthy, the nation alert; the retainers, provided with drink, do as I bid." (1228–31.)

It seems to me that anyone who from experience or intimate report knew the world of Æthelfrith, Edwin, and Ethelberga or Egbert, Hlothere, and Edric would understand Wealhtheow readily enough. Had such a man been able to quote Shakespeare, he might have said, "the lady doth protest — or profess — too much"; but he would have spoken with sympathy. If she is really sure of Hrothulf's attitude, why need she entreat Beowulf so earnestly in behalf of her sons? Indeed, *if* she is sure, why mention Hrothulf's expected conduct at all? The truth, of course, is that she is *not* sure. Like any man or woman of seventh- or eighth-century England, she has known or known of too many powerful uncles who thrust aside their princely but insecure nephews. However glorious the present, the future is uncertain and dangerous. If it is not improper to say so of a queen, Wealhtheow is partly whistling in the dark and partly putting out feelers for help. As to Beowulf, when he eventually takes account of her appeal, he is polite, even complimentary — but, I think, prudently reticent. He says only that Hrethric will be welcome at the Geatish court — doubtless either as tourist or political refugee — adding a quasi-proverbial remark to the effect that a good man makes a good visitor.

Let us recognize, now, what the poet has done for us in this narrative sequence within the larger episode of the hero's adventure at Heorot. In these scenes he has dramatized situations and relationships likely to occur often enough in his world and the world of his audience or reader. Think of the unnumbered anxious but unrecorded queens and princes here endowed with vicarious speech and representation. A few have been mentioned; there must have been very many more. To be sure, the poet was telling a story of Denmark in the early sixth century — perhaps legend, perhaps history, probably a mixture of both. But that does not impair its relevance and validity for eighth- or ninth-century England.

Tangentially related to this theme of usurpation is the status of joint or shared or sub kingship. Here too *Beowulf* and Bede are reciprocally illuminating. In a well-known scene in the poem the hero, victorious over Grendel and Grendel's dam, has returned from Denmark to the court of his uncle Hygelac, king of the Geats. The step which Hygelac now takes is not completely clear — to the modern reader — from the poem itself. This is the passage: "[Hygelac] gave him seven thousand, a hall and a throne."

> . . . him gesealde   seofan þusendo,
> bold ond bregostol.   (2195–96)

Seven thousand *what?* The poem continues: "The land, the native ancestral domain in that nation was common inheritance to them both together; broad sovereignty belonged primarily to the one of higher rank" — that is, to Hygelac.

> Him wæs bam samod
> on ðam leodscipe   lond gecynde,
> eard eðelriht,   oðrum swiðor
> side rice   þam ðær selra wæs.   (2196–99)

As has long been known, this context indicates that Hygelac gave Beowulf seven thousand *hides* — from Old English *hid*, apparently the land necessary to maintain a single family or household. The Latin term was *familia*. Bede reports similar gifts in various passages. For example, he says that King Oswy gave Peada, his brother-in-law, the domain of South Mercia, "five thousand households" (regnum . . . familiarum quinque millium), separated by the river Trent from North Mercia, which was a territory "of seven thousand households" (terra . . . familiarum septem millium).

(*H. E.* 3.24.) Bede's evidence, along with other historical references, of course, thus enables us to gauge the scope and significance
of the grant which Beowulf received from his uncle. For, whatever the conditions may have been in early sixth-century Geat-
land, the poet was surely thinking in terms of his England. So
viewed, it was a very substantial grant; and the poet's language
makes the fact of joint kingship quite definite.

In this light, and in the light of numerous references in Bede's
History, it has been plausibly suggested that Hrothulf may have
shared rule with his uncle, Hrothgar. (Klaeber, 3rd edn., p. xxxii.)
Such royal partnerships may well have facilitated aggression or
usurpation, but according to the ethics of the poem — and, I think,
of pre-Alfredian England — they did not authorize or justify it.
In both alike there was apparently no doubt who was the junior
partner and hence subordinate to the senior. In the language —
the characteristically English term — of the poem, it was clear
which was *selra*, "better" — that is, who had priority. The treatment of the matter of succession is decisive in the poem. On the
one hand, the poet's sympathy allies him — and us — with Hrothgar's young son Hrethric over whose future the powerful Hrothulf casts a threatening shadow. And on the other hand, the author
emphasizes his hero Beowulf's refusal to replace Hygelac's son
Heardred even when the situation might have appeared to justify
him fully. King Hygelac, evidently in the prime of his life, had
been killed while on a foreign campaign. His widow, Hygd, did
not believe that their young son "could protect his native land"
against possible enemies. She offered the kingship to Beowulf.
Hear the words of the poet: ". . . On no consideration could those
desolate ones obtain from that noble that he would be lord to
Heardred or that he would choose the kingship; however, he protected him [that is, Beowulf protected Heardred] with friendly advice, willingly, kindly, until he grew older, until he [actually] ruled
the Geats." (2373–78.)

So the poet reveals himself as a firm legitimist. I believe that
Bede was of the same persuasion. At any rate, the account of the
Kentish affair of Hlothere, and of the events preceding and fol-

lowing his reign, points that way. Bede is content when Wictred, "the lawful king," the son of Egbert — who had actually been succeeded by his (usurping?) brother Hlothere — achieves power.

We are all acquainted with the textbook generalization that goes like this, with allowance for variation in phrasing: In the Germanic nations the kingship was not strictly hereditary. No doubt this represents the actual course of events with objective accuracy. Many an unlucky prince saw a more aggressive or opportunistic rival pop in, like Claudius, between the election and his hopes. Yet, on the joint authority of *Beowulf* and Bede, should we be wrong to infer the emergence in eighth-century England of a party, or a body of opinion, in favor of legitimacy?

I shall not undertake to compare the views of our two authors on the kingly office as a whole. As for *Beowulf*, the topic has received considerable attention elsewhere. As for Bede, the portrait of an ideal secular ruler never engages him centrally. Nevertheless, there are more or less incidental expressions of attitude in the two works that are worth noting because of their similarity. In *Beowulf*, as in Old Germanic poetry generally, generosity, openhanded gift-giving, especially as a reward of valor, is strongly approved, and its opposite, tightfisted avarice, is condemned. It is interesting, though not surprising, to find Bede praising the rulers he most admires for their liberality. Thus both Oswald — the Northumbrian king canonized not long after his death in battle — and Oswin, sub-king of Deira, are described as generous ("largus"), Oswald to the poor and to pilgrims and Oswin to high and low alike ("nobilibus simul atque ignobilibus"). (Oswald, *H. E.* 3.6; Oswin, 3.14.) Incidentally, in the case of Oswald, the preceding paragraph comments on his earthly prosperity as well — a connection common enough in *Beowulf*, where, we may observe, generosity is regarded rather as the cause than as the effect of a ruler's success.

We might expect a religious historian to laud humility in a king, and Bede does so — when he has a chance, which was apparently not often. Thus Oswald was not only generous but always humble and kindly ("semper humilis, benignus et largus" — *H. E.* 3.6).

As for Oswin, humility was his most conspicuous trait, only momentarily contrasted with a secular sense of the fitness of things, as may be glimpsed in an anecdote involving the great Irish missionary bishop Aidan. As an aid in his constant travel, Oswin gave Aidan a fine horse ("equum optimum"). Not long afterward, Aidan encountered a poor man who asked alms. In his carefree, Celtic way, Aidan promptly dismounted and handed over the horse, regally caparisoned as it was ("ita ut erat stratus regaliter") to the beggar. When king and bishop next met at dinner, Oswin remonstrated: could not Aidan have given the man some other, ordinary beast instead of that royal horse ("equum regium") which Oswin had intended for Aidan's own use? Unworldly the bishop may have been, but not unready with his answer: "Is that son of a mare dearer to you than this son of God?" ("Numquid tibi carior est ille filius equae quam ille filius Dei?" — *H. E.* 3.14). After thinking the matter over for a few minutes, Oswin apologized profusely to Aidan and they were cheerfully reconciled. But now Aidan in turn thought things over and presently dissolved in tears. Speaking to his chaplain in their native Gaelic, he explained: he was sure that Oswin could not be long for this world, for he had never before seen a humble king. And so it turned out, as Bede had, in fact, already related: Oswin was betrayed and slain by a disloyal thane at the instigation of his cousin Oswy. Oswy, king of Northumbria and actually ruler of the area Bernicia, it would seem, could not tolerate coexistence with the sub-king Oswin, ruler of the other Northumbrian area, Deira. (*H. E.* 3.14.) In short, this was another homicidal feud within a royal family, like so many noted and lamented in *Beowulf* and Bede alike. Our poet's original audience would probably have shared Oswin's chagrin about the horse. Prominent among the rewards given by Hrothgar to Beowulf for his conquest of Grendel are eight royal horses, with ornamented headgear (fætedhleore), one of them with the king's military saddle, handsomely decorated. (1035–41.) If our own common sense is not enough, such a context highlights the egregious unworldliness of the Irish missionary against the background of Germanic and Anglo-Saxon secular values.

Both poet and historian censure the opposite of humility — excessive pride or arrogance — when it leads to disastrous acts of aggression in the relations between nations. The first reference to Hygelac's death on his expedition against the Frisians tells us that "fate took him off, after he because of pride asked for trouble, a quarrel with the Frisians":

> hyne wyrd fornam,
> syþðan he for wlenco   wean ahsode,
> fæhðe to Frysum.   (1205–7)

At somewhat greater length Bede recounts the attack of Ecgfrith, king of Northumbria, upon Ireland in the year 684. The Irish were not harming him, instead had been friendly to the English. Ravaged without cause, the Irish pronounced a curse upon Ecgfrith; and it was believed that his defeat and death the next year at Nechtansmere, in his campaign against the Picts, came as a just retribution. (*H. E.* 4.26.) Warnings against arrogance and avarice are, of course, conspicuous in Hrothgar's long speech addressed to the young Beowulf after his victory over Grendel and his mother (1700–84). And in the funeral eulogy at the end of the poem the mourners declare that Beowulf was "the mildest and gentlest of kings in the world [or] of men, the kindest to his people":

> wyruldcyning[a]
> manna mildust   ond mon (ðw) ærust,
> leodum liðost . . .   (3180–82)

Yet we misrepresent the hero if we remember only his benignity and forget his strength, strength available for other uses besides the quelling of monsters. In his farewell speech he tells his people, indeed, that he has not sought hostile intrigues or sworn false oaths. But he also says: "I held [that is, ruled and protected] this nation fifty years; there was no tribal king, none of the surrounding peoples, that dared attack me with allies, threaten with terror. I lived out my portion of time on earth, held my own well . . ."

> Ic ðas leode heold
> fiftig wintra;   næs se folccyning,
> ymbesittendra   ænig ðara,
> þe mec guðwinum   gretan dorste,

egesan ðeon.   Ic on earde bad
   mælgesceafta,   heold min tela . . .   (2732–37)

Proper enough, one might say, in a secular poem; but surely anything of this kind is not to be expected from a monastic historian? Well, Bede tells us how the good and pious King Sigbert, of Essex, was assassinated by his own men in the year 653. The assassins offered no motive except that they were angered because the king spared his enemies excessively and too easily forgot injuries done him on petition of the offenders. Thus he lost his life by obeying the gospel. Nevertheless, says Bede, the fault was genuine; in fact, one of the killers had been just such an offender. (*H. E.* 3.22.) To be sure, the offense Bede has in mind involved Christian matrimonial laws. Still, I think Bede would have us recognize that, however admirable the virtue of humility, a king should be "not too tame neither."

In this connection we should observe the favorable mood and tone in Bede's account of Æthelfrith, the early Northumbrian king already mentioned. He was a very valiant man ("fortissimus") and most desirous of fame ("gloriae cupidissimus"). He so far surpassed the other English leaders in devastating the native Celtic population that he might be compared with King Saul — except that Æthelfrith did not know the true God. Enforcing the comparison, Bede quotes with apparent approval Genesis 49:27: "Benjamin shall ravin as a wolf: in the morning he shall devour the prey, and at night he shall divide the spoil." (King James version; Bede's text reads: "Beniamin lupus rapax, mane comedet praedam, et vespere dividet spolia.") As students of the poem have long recognized, the author of *Beowulf* uses a less direct technique in magnifying his hero by implied association with great figures of Germanic legend; but the basic method is psychologically similar. As for the pursuit of fame, that, of course, permeates the motivation of heroic action in the poem. I will cite a single example. Preparing to go and avenge Æschere, devoured by Grendel's mother, Beowulf says to Hrothgar: "let him who may achieve fame before death; that is afterward best for a warrior no longer living."

  . . .   wyrce se þe mote
domes ær deaþe; þæt bið drihtguman
unlifgendum æfter selest. (1387–89)

In quoting from the final eulogy of Beowulf himself above, I omitted the last adjective, which happens also to be the last word of the poem. His mourners declare the hero not only the mildest and gentlest and kindest of kings and men but also "the most desirous of praise," "lofgeornost." (3182.) Since the characterization throughout the poem excludes any merely absurb vanity, "lofgeornost" implies eagerness to do deeds worthy of praise. In Beowulf's situation, such deeds would be acts of bravery or of generosity. Klaeber, the editor of the poem, cites Bede's designation of Æthelfrith which I have quoted above — "gloriae cupidissimus" — and notes that in the Alfredian translation of Bede it is rendered as "gylpgeornesta" ("most eager for glory"). Thus converge or coincide attitudes and ideals from the Germanic Heroic Age, from the early eighth-century church historian, from the late ninth-century court of Wessex — and from our undated poem.

 I can mention certain minor matters only briefly. Celebrating the success and prosperity of his Christian convert hero, Edwin of Northumbria, Bede relates that he had such splendor in his kingdom ("tantum . . . in regno excellentiae") that not only were banners ("vexilla") carried before him in battle, but a standard bearer ("signifer") was accustomed to precede him in his progresses through the country; even in purely local movement along the highway he had his banner — Latin *tufa*, English "tuf." (*H. E.* 2.16.) In *Beowulf*, alike in battles and at funerals, standards and banners are fairly prominent. Worth recalling, perhaps, is that Heorot, "Hart," the name of Hrothgar's hall in Denmark, has an English onomastic counterpart: "Heruteä," "Insula Cervi," Isle of the Hart is the name of the monastic house presided over by the famous abbess Hild. (*H. E.* 3.24.) Every reader of *Beowulf* remembers the horse-racing engaged in by the Danes on their joyful return from Grendel's pool, after the hero's first victory. "Sometimes competing, they traversed the fallow highway with their horses":

Beowulf *and Bede*

Hwilum flitende   fealwe stræte
mearum mæton.   (916–17)

An image of the Venerable Bede as a detailed *rapporteur,* if not an *aficionado,* of the track may seem calculated to startle slightly. But he was. The narrative concerns an event of the youth of Herebald, now — that is, approximately the year 731 — abbot of Wearmouth but once a callow pupil of Bishop John of Hexham. On one occasion the bishop and his company of students, some laymen, some intended for the clergy, were on a journey. When they came to a stretch of road flat and wide and suitable for horse racing ("viam planam et amplam aptamque cursui equorum"), the boys — especially the laymen — begged the bishop to let them have a go at it. He gave in, excepting only Herebald from permission. Herebald, of course, pleaded hard but to no avail. As the racing continued, apparently for some time, he could no longer contain himself and joined in the contest anyway. But alas, presently his spirited ("fervens") horse suddenly jumped a low spot and pitched Herebald on the ground. He landed on the only rock in the vicinity, broke his thumb, cracked his skull, and lay unconscious for several hours. (*H. E.* 5.6.) Bishop John's subsequent care and prayer effected a miraculous recovery — and this, of course, was Bede's motive in telling the story. The author's edifying purpose, however, does not impair the value of the narrative as evidence. We observe that this bit of racing was casual, "amateur," and incidental to a journey — just as in *Beowulf.* Here, as in many other matters large and small, the poet did not have to rely on ancient traditions from the Continent. He could draw on his experience and observation of contemporary life in England.

Let us turn, finally, to an episode of the year 679 involving the royal families of Ecgfrith of Northumbria and Ethelred of Mercia. This is Bede's account (*H. E.* 4.21): "The ninth year of the reign of Ecgfrith a hard battle was fought between him and Ethelred, king of Mercia, by the river Trent, in which was slain Elfwine, king Ecgfrith's brother, a young man of about eighteen years and well beloved by both countries. For his sister too, named Osthryth, was wife to king Ethelred. And whereas there seemed to have arisen an occasion of sharper war and longer enmity between the fierce kings and peoples, Theodore the bishop, beloved of God, making use of divine help, by his wholesome exhortation quenched the fire of so great a peril — in such a way that, the kings and people being pacified on both sides, the life of no man perished for the death of the king's brother, but only a due sum of money was given to the king that was the avenger." (Translation by Stapleton.)

Several features of this succinct narrative sound notes familiar to the reader of *Beowulf*: the blood feud, along with its role in actual war, and the possibility of settlement by money; marriage as an instrument of foreign policy; and the tragic situation of the lady Osthryth, whose young brother Elfwine was slain by her husband Ethelred's men — if not, indeed, by Ethelred himself.

The "avenger" (*ultor*) of Bede's account is, of course, King Ecgfrith of Northumbria. His brother, Elfwine, was killed by a Mercian or Mercians; therefore Ecgfrith would quite normally be expected to dispatch either Elfwine's slayer, or an important member of his family or, at all events, a prominent man affiliated with the party that slew Elfwine. This was the standard Germanic code; Miss Dorothy Whitelock (in *The Audience of Beowulf*) has shown that it was followed long after the advent of Christianity in England. To take only one example from the poem, Beowulf himself tells how he slew Dæghrefn on the expedition in which Hygelac lost his life, quite probably at the hands of this same Dæghrefn. (2501–8.) However, for the man who had the obligation of exacting vengeance there was an alternative — recognized, ancient, and honorable. Like Ecgfrith in our story, he could accept an adequate payment from the slayer or from his family or friends. The Anglo-Saxon law codes, in fact, fix a scale of values — not to call it a price list — ranging from king down to slave. This was known as wergeld, "payment for a man." Although Christian influence was doubtless exerted in favor of this alternative to blood vengeance, wergeld is far older than Christianity in the Germanic world. The Icelandic family sagas, dealing with life in the pre-Christian tenth century primarily, record its abundant employment. It is prominent in our poem too. Again, I will mention only one instance.

116

Beowulf's father, Ecgtheow, had killed a man of the Wilfing clan or family in a feud: to prevent further turmoil, he came to the court of Hrothgar, king of the Danes. Hrothgar, the pagan or secular equivalent of the archbishop Theodore in Bede's narrative, acted as mediator. I will quote only the concluding part of Hrothgar's fourteen-line account: "Then I settled the quarrel with money; I sent ancient treasures over the ridge of water to the Wilfings; he [Ecgtheow] swore oaths to me (i.e., to keep the peace henceforth)."

> Siððan þa fæhðe   feo þingode;
> sende ic Wylfingum   ofer wæteres hrycg
> ealde madmas;   he me aþas swor.   (470–72)

Returning to Bede now, we were told that Ecgfrith's and Elfwine's sister Osthryth was the wife of the Mercian king Ethelred. This marriage doubtless played a part in a political arrangement; it may have represented an alliance between Northumbria and Mercia; or perhaps it was intended to compose a difference between two royal houses. If so, it was evidently not a lasting success. The poem, again, offers a parallel. During Beowulf's visit at King Hrothgar's court he learned of the betrothal of Freawaru, daughter of Hrothgar, to Ingeld, the young king (or king to be) of the Heatho-Bards. He explains the design to Hygelac: "The lord of the Scyldings, protector of the realm, has arranged this, and counts it a good plan that he may with this woman settle a number of deadly feuds [and] quarrels." But Beowulf is skeptical of the outcome; he adds: "Seldom does the slaying spear rest, even for a little while — after a leader's fall — even though the bride be excellent." (2024–31.) And he goes on to conjecture a vivid scene in which the spark of old enmity will be rekindled. He pictures the Danish bride and her Danish escorts as they come into the Heatho-Bard hall; some of these Danes will carry weapons and wear ornaments taken from dead Heatho-Bards — Heatho-Bards slain in the quarrel to which this marriage is designed to put an end. Let the poet take it from here:

"Then an old spearman will speak over the beer, one who catches sight of an ornament, one who remembers everything, the slaughter of men (and all) — he has a savage spirit; he begins to try out the mind of a young champion, to awaken the evil of war; and he speaks these words: 'My friend, can you recognize the sword, the one your father carried to battle — excellent weapon — the last time, where the Danes slew him . . . ? Now the son of one or another of those slayers walks upon the floor here, exulting in his armor, boasts of the killing, and wears that treasure which by right you ought to have.' Thus [the old man] prompts and reminds him on every occasion with bitter words, until the time comes when the lady's escort — for his father's deeds — lies blood-stained after the bite of a sword, his life forfeited. . . ." The avenging Heatho-Bard will steal away; but now pledges will be broken on both sides; Ingeld will be estranged from his wife; and war will be renewed between Danes and Heatho-Bards. (2041ff.)

History — Bede's *History*, at all events — does not tell us just how the war broke out between Northumbrians and Mercians. And usually it is poetry rather than history that offers us scenes like the one we have been looking at in *Beowulf*. But some of the material circumstances and even more of the motivations, feelings, and impulses depicted by the poet must have figured in many a crisis at many an Anglo-Saxon court. Bede mentions the "fierce" ("feroces") natures of kings and peoples alike and makes clear Ecgfrith's initial resolution to seek blood vengeance for Elfwine, the young prince regarded as "very likable" ("multum amabilis") by both nations. Bede *tells* us, the poet *shows* us how the code of private vengeance could lead to public war.

Now, at last, let us consider Osthryth, sister of the slain Elfwine and wife of Ethelred, king of his Mercian slayers. Of all those involved, her anguish must have been the most bitter because her emotions were utterly divided — between grief for her brother and loyalty to her husband. Bede, of course, says nothing about this, merely recording that she was the sister of one man and the wife of the other. Historians generally, and medieval historians especially, seldom venture into the realm of subjective experience — except for visions and dreams. Besides, Elfwine's plight was frequent enough in Germanic life. But literature steps in to fill the gap. To be sure, Osthryth had no poet to lament her fate; or, if she did, the work has not come down to us. But there is a queen in *Beowulf* whose tragic position is almost identical, or rather, even more poignant. In this story Hildeburg, a Danish princess, is the wife of a king whose name is Finn; he rules over the Frisians or Jutes; they have a young son of military age. Hildeburg's brother, Hnæf, and a company of Danes have come, apparently on a visit, to Finn's court. In some way a deadly battle breaks out at night between Danes and Frisians (or Jutes). Both Hnæf and the son of Finn and Hildeburg are killed — fighting on opposite sides, presumably. In the poet's rendering our attention is focused primarily on Hildeburg; after three opening lines which identify the story he continues thus: "Hildeburg, indeed, had no need to praise the faith of the Jutes; guiltless, she was bereft of dear ones at that shield-play, of son(s) and brother(s); wounded by the spear, they fell to their fate; that was a sorrowful lady! Not without cause did Hoc's daughter [Hildeburg] mourn her destiny, after morning came, when she could see the evil slaughter — where before she had had the greatest happiness in the world." (1071–80.) After giving the terms of a truce between the survivors, the poet devotes eighteen verses to the common funeral pyre on which the dead from both sides are burned. Here too Hildeburg's position is central. "Then Hildeburg commanded them to commit her own son to the flame on Hnæf's pyre, to place him beside his uncle on the fire. The lady lamented, uttered her grief in chants." (1114–18.)

By way of footnote, there is a violent sequel to each of these tales of unhappy queens. The *Beowulf* poet tells us how the Danes later attacked in force, slew king Finn, and carried Hildeburg back home to Denmark. (1138–59.) And Bede, citing the occurrence as the event of the year 697 — nearly two decades after the Northumbrian-Mercian war — notes that Osthryth was murdered (*interempta*) by her Mercian nobles. (*H. E.* 5.24.)

The conclusion toward which I am drawing is doubtless already evident. The deliberately paced reader of *Beowulf* — and all readers of the poem in Old English pace deliberately — feels both its depth and its immediacy. Like the much shorter *Battle of Maldon*, it is three-dimensional — to a degree far beyond most Old English narrative poems. This convincing human significance pervades the entire work, including everything from plot, characterization, and "digressions" to appositely cited proverbs. Its density and richness derive from its intimate relationship to contemporary life. Not forgetting that he was a Trojan prince, Chaucer makes his Troilus a medieval knight. Shakespeare, doubtless aware that Hamlet was a house-burning Scandinavian avenger, presents him as a Renaissance intellectual. The *Beowulf* poet took his plots, his episodes, and his "'digressions" from Germanic tradition. But he clothed these bones with the flesh and blood, the mind and heart of his own time. The portrait of the hero fits the highest ethical ideal of the age; it could scarcely have been drawn very differently by Bede himself. Beowulf is as steadily wise and good as he is strong. He is neither infallible nor all-powerful. That is one reason, I think, why we believe in him, accept him as "real," in an appropriate meaning of the word. The other reason is the world — the human world — in which he lives and acts. That world has the variety of life itself — life in Anglo-Saxon England, with its peculiar mixture of good and bad within and among men, of trust and treachery, of predictable and unpredictable. For independent testimony about the milieu of hero and poet we turn to history: to the *Old English Annals* and other sources — but above all to the masterly work of Bede.

And now a very brief epilogue.

Our Queen Osthryth, unlike Hildeburg, did not mourn her brother beside a funeral pyre. All her people were Christian, so doubtless Elfwine received orthodox rites. Yet, musing over the Sutton Hoo ship burial — or rather cenotaphic memorial — put down only a few decades earlier in East Anglia, one may briefly indulge a fleeting fancy. Might not a similar commemoration have been bestowed upon an attractive and popular young prince, brother and brother-in-law of the two most powerful kings in the England of that time? I shall not urge my readers to form parties of amateur archaeologists and spend a summer digging — perhaps along a Mercian-Northumbrian boundary river — for Elfwine's ship. For all that, it could just possibly be there!

We are on more solid ground when we align Sutton Hoo with the funerals described in *Beowulf*. There are three: Hnæf's, which we have noted — a funeral pyre; Scyld's, at the beginning of the poem — here a ship bearing the body and rich trappings, not buried but launched on the open sea; and that of the hero, Beowulf — cremation on a pyre followed by the erection of a memorial beacon. Together they fill more than a hundred lines of the poem; each is a vivid and striking scene. This indicates the interest of the poet and inferentially of his audience — interest in the customs of the past; and, since Sutton Hoo, we must say not merely of the Continental but of the insular past as well. Written history is almost totally silent about these things; they were heathen in origin, and the ecclesiastical writers were self-consciously Christian. Hence it is that old poets and new archaeologists collaborate in supplementing the record transmitted to us by historians — even such excellent ones as St. Bede.

⟩ T. J. OLESON ⟨

VIKING—TUNNIT—ESKIMO

By 800 Western Europe had reached, relatively speaking, a condition of some stability and peace. The Merovingian dynasty had been replaced by the Carolingian, and the Moslem incursions from Spain into Gaul had been stopped. The Saxons had been incorporated into the Frankish state and were in the process of being Christianized, and the Slavic tribes beyond them posed no great threat. The Lombards in Italy had made their submission to the Frankish king and their territories formed a part of his realm; the Avar threat had been wiped out in a series of highly profitable campaigns. It is true that the Moslems remained a potential threat to the southern shores of the Mediterranean, particularly to Italy and its adjacent islands. Nevertheless, in comparison with the previous three centuries a certain tranquillity reigned and the tide of culture which had been at low ebb for the last two or three centuries was rising again in the movement popularly known as the Carolingian Renaissance. The origins of this "renaissance" are to be sought in the flourishing culture of eighth-century England, a country which although not a unitary state was relatively free from bloody tribal rivalries and boasted a high level of

NOTE. The research for this paper was in part made possible by a Faculty Research Fellowship granted by the Social Science Research Council.

scholarship and learning. Scholars were now busily engaged on the Continent in monastic foundations, in the cathedrals, and in the royal Palace School of the Frankish kings at the task of preserving, digesting, and imitating the works of the classical culture of Rome and to a lesser extent that of Greece. The "fierce" German barbarians, who in the fifth and sixth centuries had settled in various parts of the western half of the Roman Empire, were being successfully assimilated into a fast-growing and vigorous Christian society.

Little as it knew it, Europe was, however, standing on the threshold of a new age of anarchy and chaos — the Viking Age. It was to be a period of violence and virility, of destruction and disaster, of exemplary endurance and shameful submission; but it was also to be a period pregnant with vital forces which, after the initial bloody onslaughts, were to express themselves creatively in every sphere of life. But first there was agony to be endured. The Moslems were to launch new and devastating attacks in the western Mediterranean. The Magyars were to occupy the great plain of Hungary and from it set out on their massive booty-gathering raids to all of Western Europe. The descendants of the great Charles were to engage in internecine warfare, crippling the power of the Carolingian dynasty and thereby contributing to the growth of feudalism with its decentralizing tendencies.[1]

Serious as all these dread demons of chaos were, they vanish almost as shadows before the mighty agents of destruction which were to descend on Western Europe in the ninth and tenth centuries. Fittingly they were spawned in the north, the part of the earth which contemporaries believed to be the home of Satan and the evil spirits who did his bidding. He who reads the Gospel, says the homilist, faces north in order to show that God's word overcomes the forces of evil, for the north symbolizes the devil.[2]

In the last decade of the eighth century there emerged from the deep fjords of Norway and the sunny sounds of Denmark the last

[1] A convenient summary of these events is Christopher Dawson, *The Making of Europe* (New York, 1932; paperback edition in Meridian Books).

[2] *Homiliu-bok*, ed. T. Wisen (Lund, 1872), p. 123.

and most terrible of the Teutonic barbarians. What brought about this sudden onslaught? The most likely answer is overpopulation, especially in Norway. The violent irruption thence was preceded and paralleled by a peaceful exodus of large numbers of Norwegians, who established themselves in the island chain north of the British Isles, the Hebrides, Orkney, Shetland, and Faroe islands. Norway has always been a country whose soil has only grudgingly yielded a meager harvest and it is not surprising that in a period of expansion and growth its resources should prove inadequate in the face of an increasing population.

The descent of the Norwegian Vikings on Western Europe antedates by some years the outburst of other Vikings from Denmark, a country whose soil is much more generous than that of Norway. The cause for the Danish raids may thus have been different. Tales of the rich booty brought back by the Norwegians may have aroused a desire for emulation on the part of the Danes. Or it may be that the violent conversion of the Saxons by Charlemagne and their political subjection aroused fears of Frankish encroachment in the hearts of the Danes and a dread that their turn would come next.[3]

Be that as it may, all the Scandinavian peoples had by the ninth century perfected ships which lent themselves ideally to hit-and-run raids on nearby countries which could be reached by coastal navigation. The longship, narrow, low-built, suited to rowing, capable of carrying from twenty to sixty warriors, was well adapted not only to coastal navigation and the crossing of moderate expanses of not too stormy waters, but also to penetration far inland on numerous rivers which could serve as highways into the interior of Western Europe and England.[4] Germany, France, Spain, England, Scotland, and Ireland became in the ninth century all too familiar with the sight of these "dragon" ships as they made their way especially to centers such as monasteries where rich booty might be expected.

[3] See A. W. Brögger, *Ancient Emigrants* (Oxford, 1929); J. Bröndsted, *The Vikings* (London, 1933).
[4] A. W. Brögger and H. Shetelig, *The Viking Ships* (Oslo, 1951).

There is no doubt that the great majority of attacks were, at least in the first half of the ninth century, booty-gathering expeditions, but even then there may have been, as there certainly were later, other motives for these overseas ventures. The Vikings have been truly designated as cruel and fierce barbarians, and indeed they showed themselves as such, but they had another side to their character. The inhabitants of Norway and Denmark in the pre-Viking period were members of communities of free-born peasants, who in Denmark led an agrarian life and in Norway subsisted by husbandry and hunting. When overpopulation and unstable political conditions in the ninth century prompted them to seek new lands overseas, they only sought to continue their traditional way of life.

It cannot be asserted that the earliest raids on England were stimulated by such a motive, but this cannot be ruled out. It may be that the Scandinavians, upon finding such rich centers of wealth as the monasteries and churches of both the British Isles and Western Europe, were for the moment diverted from their primary concern of finding new homelands to the plunder of what must have seemed to them fabulous riches. At any rate we know that after spending some years or even decades in booty-gathering expeditions, the Vikings in almost all cases turned their attention to the acquisition of permanent bases and homes in both the British Isles and the countries of Western Europe, especially Gaul or present-day France.

This process is so well known and has so often been discussed that it is unnecessary here to recount the history of the Viking incursions and settlements in Western Europe.[5] The early attacks on England in the first half of the ninth century may be described as in the main pirate raids. We are also familiar with the change of emphasis which led to an attempt to establish, with considerable success, permanent Scandinavian enclaves within the domains of the Anglo-Saxon kings, notably the territory, if we may employ that term, which came to be known as the Danelaw from the fact that among its inhabitants the law of the Danes was the

[5] See J. C. H. R. Steenstrup, *Normannerne* (Copenhagen, 1876–1882).

sovereign authority — a result of the Germanic concept of law which guaranteed to each individual the rights which were his by birth. We know also that in the legal, military, political, social, and constitutional fields the impact of the Vikings on Anglo-Saxon England was very considerable. And when these early ninth-century settlers and their descendants had been to a considerable extent assimilated in the course of the tenth century, a fresh incursion of Danes in the first four decades of the eleventh century further transformed the structure and organization of Anglo-Saxon society. It would again be superfluous to mention the enormous consequences of the Viking attacks on France in the ninth century. They were to a large extent responsible for the shattering of the somewhat exotic unity which Charlemagne, by what was really only a tour de force, had succeeded in imposing on the territories of which he had been crowned emperor by the pope on that most easily remembered of dates, Christmas day, 800. The Viking invasions of France may have made the development of feudalism inevitable in that country, but they also had even greater consequences in the evolution of two kingdoms, England and Sicily, that were the precursors of the national state of later medieval and modern times.

The conquest of Anglo-Saxon England welded the vigor and political adaptability of the Norman descendants of the Vikings to the advanced administrative competence of the Anglo-Saxons. This combination produced an efficient system of government together with feudal institutions that preserved ancient Germanic beliefs in the supremacy of law and the duty of both king and folk to maintain in cooperation if possible, in opposition if necessary, the supremacy of that law. The later evolution of both parliamentary institutions and the common law, especially the latter, owes a great deal to the Anglo-Saxon heritage which the Normans were careful to preserve. It is true that parliamentary institutions were not peculiar to Norman England and indeed developed to a certain stage in other countries, for example Spain, before dying prematurely. Only in Norman England, however, did the Germanic concept of law survive to such an extent that it fructified both the legal and the constitutional practices and procedures of the English-speaking world.

The Norman genius was to express itself in a different way in Sicily, the other kingdom that had its ultimate origin in 911 when Charles the Simple invested the Viking leader Rollo with what was to become the duchy of Normandy. Incidentally one can only admire the forbearance and far-sightedness of Charles the Simple during this embarrassing episode. The chroniclers tell us that Rollo "refused to kiss the foot of Charles when he received from him the duchy of Normandy. 'He who receives such a gift,' said the bishops to him, 'ought to kiss the foot of the king.' 'Never,' replied he, 'will I bend the knee to anyone, or kiss anybody's foot.' Nevertheless, impelled by the entreaties of the Franks, he ordered one of his warriors to perform the act in his stead. This man seized the foot of the king and lifted it to his lips, kissing it without bending and so causing the king to tumble over backwards. At that time there was a loud burst of laughter and a great commotion in the crowd of onlookers." [6] Although these same unbending Normans were ambitious and a thorn in the side of the French kings they undoubtedly contributed greatly to the process through which France became the outstanding power in thirteenth-century Europe, and it was the act of Charles the Simple that transformed the Normans from great enemies of western Christendom into its greatest champions, both in the sphere of Church reform and in the later Crusades.

The contempt for authority shown in the episode of the kissing of the foot is somewhat ironical when one considers the development of the other kingdom established by the Norman descendants of the Vikings in the eleventh century. In the years between 1016 and 1090 a handful of Normans carved out a kingdom in southern Italy against the opposition of not only petty Italian rulers but the Byzantine emperors, the Moslem rulers of Sicily, and various popes and Holy Roman emperors. Here they established a state which in its emphasis on the authority of the ruler and the subordination of the subject to the state reminds one more of Nazi

[6] F. A. Ogg, *A Source Book of Mediaeval History* (New York, 1907) , p. 172.

Germany than of any other state of modern times. The most brilliant embodiment of this absolutism was Frederick II, *stupor mundi* or "wonder of the world." He regarded himself as almost a semi-divine being, the representative on earth of necessity and justice. One can imagine what would have been the fate of one with the temerity to act toward him as Rollo did toward Charles the Simple. But Nemesis overtook Frederick. His attempt to impose his authoritarianism and economic system on the Papal States and the increasingly independent towns of northern Italy ended in disaster, and we are told that the emperor died because he neglected, or failed to realize that he was neglecting, the advice of a soothsayer. This individual had told him that he would die in Florence and that he must avoid it at all costs. This Frederick did, but in 1250 he came to Castel Fiorentino in Sicily and there in fulfillment of the prophecy he died after a short illness. At his death or shortly thereafter the kingdom that stemmed from the Vikings of Normandy passed into other hands.[7]

It is not my intention to pursue further these reflections on the history of the Vikings in Western Europe. I wish rather to discuss a less well known episode in the history of the Vikings, their expansion north and west across the Atlantic, their colonization of Greenland, and their fate in the Arctic regions of Greenland and Canada. Some portions of this episode in the history of the Vikings are well known, such as the Vinland voyages. Other and later features are less familiar and I wish to discuss them at some length.

The peaceful exodus from Norway to the island chain north of Scotland in the late eighth and the ninth centuries was followed by a further and much greater migration from Norway in the last half of the ninth century when Harald the Fairhaired was seeking to make himself sole king of the Norwegians. Some time after 850 the Norwegians both at home and in the British Isles became aware of the existence of a large island in the North Atlantic. Whether they learned of it by being accidentally driven off course to it or whether they heard of it from the Irish who had long been

[7] E. Kantorowicz, *Frederick II* (London, 1931).

aware of it is not known. Some Irish priests had established themselves there possibly even earlier than the eighth century and carried on their ascetic way of life under the midnight sun, which, we
are told, was bright enough to allow them to pick the lice off their
shirts.[8] At any rate the Norwegians began settlement of the island
shortly after 870, taking with them enough Irish slaves or retainers so that today the blood of the Icelanders is estimated to be at
least 30 per cent Irish.[9]

The island to which was given the inhospitable name of Iceland was then, we are told, fully settled in the next sixty years.
Iceland lies halfway between Europe and America. Its discovery
made inevitable the discovery of the latter. Ships driven off course
west of Iceland could easily sight the mountains on the east coast
of Greenland, which indeed can on occasion be seen by abnormal
refraction from the west coast mountains of Iceland. Preoccupied,
however, with the problems of settling a new country and blessed
with abundant land to begin with, the Icelanders made no attempt for a hundred years to visit, let alone settle, Greenland. It
is true that at some time in the first decades of the ninth century
a certain Gunnbjorn Ulfsson was driven off course and sighted
either the mountain peaks of east Greenland or islands off Ang-
magssalik, which though never definitely located were henceforth
known as the Skerries of Gunnbjorn. Again around 980 some Icelanders spent a winter on the icy east coast of Greenland but
without any lasting result.

In 982 a citizen of the Icelandic commonwealth, Eirikr Thor-
valdsson, commonly known as Eric the Red, was sentenced to
three years' outlawry for homicide. Spurred, it would seem, by reports of the vast land west of Iceland, he decided to spend his
three years' sentence in exploring this country. It is not without
significance that Eric and his father, who had come to Iceland after being convicted of homicide, had lived on various farms of
poor quality where only a meager living could be made. Eric may

[8] Dicuil, *Liber de mensura orbis terrae* (Berlin, 1870), pp. 42–44.
[9] On the discovery and settlement of Iceland see Jón Jóhannesson, *Íslendinga
saga* (Reykjavik, 1956–1958), I, 11–49.

have been looking for "greener pastures." At any rate he spent the
three years of his outlawry exploring the west coast of Greenland
and found there many hospitable fjords covered in summer with
lush vegetation, and in many cases no less attractive than many
of the better parts of Iceland. He decided to settle in this land.

He returned to Iceland in 985 and reported his discovery of a
new land to which he gave, for propaganda purposes we are told,
the enticing name of Greenland. A colonization venture was
launched and in 986 Eric led a flotilla of 25 ships, 14 of which
reached the west coast of Greenland, the other 11 being either lost
or driven back to Iceland. In the next few years two settlements
arose on the west coast. These were to be known as the Eastern
Settlement, around present-day Julianehaab, and the Western
Settlement, in the vicinity of the Godthaab fjords.[10]

What attracted the Icelanders to Greenland was not only the
possibility of following an economy based, as in Iceland and Norway, on husbandry, supplemented by hunting, but even more the
great abundance of game. There were herds of reindeer in the interior; whales, walrus, narwhal, and bears in the sea and on the
ice north of the colonies. Eider ducks were also to be found in the
northern regions, and polar foxes and white falcons particularly
on Baffin Island. Voyages to the west of Davis Strait and north
and west of Baffin Bay must have begun as soon as the Icelandic
colonies in Greenland were established. These voyages were
known as Nordrsetuferdir and these districts as Nordrseta (northern "sitter's" region).[11]

Voyages to the east coast of America also began early. According to one source, Newfoundland and the shores of Labrador and
Baffin Island were sighted by a certain Bjarni Herjolfsson in the
very year in which the first settlers arrived in Greenland. According to another source Leif the son of Eric the Red landed in three

[10] On the discovery of Greenland see *ibid.*, pp. 121–125; Jón Duason, *Land-
könnun og Landnám Islendinga í Vesturheimi* (Reykjavik, 1941–1947), pp. 53–82.
On the Skerries of Gunnbjorn see H. Hermannsson, *Jón Gudmundsson and His
Natural History of Iceland,* Islandica XV (Ithaca, N.Y., 1924), pp. 29–31.

[11] On the economy and culture of Greenland in the Middle Ages see Jóhannesson, *Íslendinga saga,* I, 359–488.

regions known as Vinland (Wineland, possibly the New England coast), Markland (Woodland, some portion of the forested part of Labrador), and Helluland (Flagstoneland, no doubt Baffin Island) in the year 1000. Among other voyages was a colonization venture by an Icelander named Thorfinnr Karlsefni who came to Greenland shortly after the year 1000 and there married the widow of one of the sons of Eric the Red. He spent two or three years somewhere on the east coast of America between New York and the Gulf of St. Lawrence. The data supplied by the two sagas, *Eiriks saga rauda* and *Graenlendinga saga*, that describe the voyages are so vague, confused, and sometimes contradictory that it has proved impossible to localize Vinland, although it is not for lack of trying on the part of scholars. Vinland has been located, for example, on the west coast of Greenland by a scholar who thought the Icelandic colonies there were to be found on the east coast; it has been located in James Bay on the hypothesis that the climate had been much warmer around the year 1000 than it is at present; it has been located on the Great Lakes; it has also been located in Florida and in many other spots. The truth of the matter is that any attempt to locate Vinland will be futile until archaeological research has uncovered some evidence of the site of the colony. So far none has been found in a locality which has the mild winter climate which both sagas agree characterized Vinland.[12]

In 1961, however, the Norwegian explorer and author Helge Ingstad found some house ruins at L'Anse-aux-Meadows on the northern tip of Newfoundland which he thought might be houses the Icelanders built there. In 1962 further excavations were carried out at this site. These revealed that the houses might be but were not necessarily Norse structures from the Middle Ages. Very few artifacts were found, only some iron nails and quantities of slag, which showed that iron had been smelted there. No final report has appeared but Carbon 14 tests appear to suggest a date in

---

[12] On the Vinland voyages see *ibid.*, pp. 186–242; John R. Swanton, *The Wineland Voyages*, Smithsonian Miscellaneous Collections, CVII, No. 12 (Washington, D.C., 1947).

the neighborhood of 1000. Claims have been made that this was the site of Vinland but the climate of northern Newfoundland is such that it can in no sense fit that of the Vinland described in the sagas, and the grapes from which Wineland got its name are not to be found there. Various attempts have been made to get around these objections. It has been suggested that there were two Vinlands, a northern and a southern one. It has been contended that *vin* in Vinland means not wine but meadows, a suggestion that is philologically unsound and indeed irreconcilable with all references to Vinland from the earliest mention of it in a literary work, Adam of Bremen's *History of the Archbishops of Hamburg-Bremen*, written about 1070. Some believe that the climate of northern Newfoundland has deteriorated greatly since the year 1000 but there is no evidence that this is so. Indeed it remains a fact that if one is to place any reliance on the accounts of the Vinland voyages given in the two major sources, the most likely location of it is on Cape Cod or its environs where, however, in spite of a good deal of amateur archaeological work, no trustworthy evidence has been found.[13]

We do not know how many voyages were made to Vinland. The two sagas record only those made by people who were either members of, or connected with, the family of Eric the Red. There is no reason to believe that there may not have been others. But there can be little doubt that no real attempt was made except by Thorfinnr Karlsefni to found colonies there, an attempt he abandoned because of the hostility of the natives, whether these were Indians or remote ancestors of the present-day Eskimo. Even the location of Vinland may have been forgotten, for we are told that in 1121 a certain bishop sailed from Greenland in search of it.[14]

The Vinland voyages have, in short, exercised such a fascination on all who study them that in many cases their judgment has become beclouded and their imagination has run riot. What was only a fleeting and unimportant episode in the history of the Vikings

[13] H. Ingstad, "Discovery of Vinland," *Arctic Circular*, XI (1963); *Landet under Leidarstjernen* (Oslo, 1959), pp. 245–272.

[14] *Annalar og Nafnaskrá*, ed. Gudni Jónsson (Reykjavik, 1948), *sub anno* 1121.

has been made to appear something spectacular, dramatic, and consequential. This has been done, too, at the expense of the history of the really important sphere of activity of the Vikings in America, i.e., the history of the five hundred years which the Vikings spent in Greenland, Labrador, Hudson Bay, and the islands of the Canadian Arctic. This was a period during which the Vikings gradually lost their language, their religion, and to a considerable extent their physical identity. Let us briefly examine this.

Until the close of the fifteenth century communications were maintained between the Icelandic colonies in Greenland and the mother country and Scandinavia. After 1262 when Iceland and its colonies in Greenland accepted the king of Norway as their personal sovereign, Greenland came more and more to depend on Norway for its contact with the outside world. This was partly due to the decline of Icelandic shipping in the thirteenth century and to the increasing monopolistic commercial system which the Norwegian crown enforced on its tributary lands. After the middle of the fourteenth century only ships licensed by the crown could sail to Iceland or Greenland and direct sailings between these two lands were forbidden.[15]

The ties which bound Greenland to the outside world were those of religion and trade. Christianity, of course, became the religion of Greenland when it was adopted by the Icelandic Althing in the year 1000 and shortly thereafter Thjodhildr, the wife of Eric the Red, built the first Christian church to be erected in the Western Hemisphere. The ruins of this were only discovered in 1961. It was a very small and unassuming structure.[16] Christianity, however, spread throughout the settlements and although the population of the settlements was small — variously estimated at 3,000–10,000 — Greenland was made an episcopal diocese in 1124 with the cathedral church located at Gardar. Tithes were paid to Rome chiefly in walrus tusks and ropes made from walrus hides,

---

[15] Jóhannesson, *Íslendinga saga*, II, 147–153; Duason, *Landkönnun*, pp. 1209–1335.

[16] M. Wolfe, "Thjodhild's Church," *American Scandinavian Review*, LI (1963), 55–66.

and bishops were regularly appointed until the time of the Refor-
mation, but ceased to reside in Greenland after 1378. Why this was
so is a mystery.[17]

Trade was also an important tie with Europe. The Greenlanders needed or desired certain products unobtainable in their country. Wheat and barley were probably imported in limited quantities. The same possibly applies to the importation of timber to
supplement the driftwood found especially on the coasts of Greenland north of the settlements. The bulk of timber, however, was
no doubt obtained from Labrador. A ship that had gone there from
Greenland was driven to Iceland in 1378.[18]

But the most important and necessary import from Europe was
iron. Throughout their existence the Eastern and Western Settlements seemed to have been supplied with at least the minimal
requirements of iron necessary for husbandry and even to have
supplied iron to the hunters who early took up abodes in the game-
rich areas of the Arctic north and west of the farming settlements.[19] It is evident, however, that iron was never in plentiful
supply in spite of the fact that the Greenlanders produced a small
amount of bog iron. In ruins dating from the very early days of the
settlement stone and bone implements have been found attesting
to the limited quantity of iron available.[20]

To pay for these imports the Greenlanders possessed several
articles much sought after and highly prized in Europe. First and
foremost were the tusks and the hide of the walrus. The ivory of
medieval Europe used in the carving of various articles was not
for some centuries primarily that of the elephant but that of the
walrus. The ropes made from the hide of this animal were, because
of their great strength, admirably suited for the rigging of ships.[21]

[17] Paul Nörlund, *Viking Settlers in Greenland* (London, 1963), pp. 28–54.
[18] *Grönlands historiske Mindesmaerker* (Copenhagen, 1838–1845), III, 14; Duason, *Landkönnun*, pp. 1340–1344.
[19] See Duason, *Landkönnun*, pp. 416–421.
[20] Niels Nielsen, *Evidence on the Extraction of Iron in Greenland by the Norse-
men*, Meddelelser om Grönland, LXXVI (Copenhagen, 1930); *Evidence of Iron
Extraction at Sandnes*, Meddelelser om Grönland, LXXXVIII, No. 4 (Copenhagen, 1936).
[21] *The King's Mirror*, tr. L. M. Larson (New York, 1917), pp. 140–141; *Kul-*

In addition the head of these "whale horses" seems to have exercised a fascination on medieval man. In 1276 King Magnus Hakonarson of Norway presented King Edward I of England with the head of a walrus complete with tusks.[22] In the churchyard of the cathedral church at Gardar in Greenland some thirty walrus heads lacking tusks were found buried and a few in the church itself.[23]

Useful also for carving was the tooth or horn of that strange creature the narwhal. These horns were exported to Europe where they seem to have been prized especially for their medicinal qualities as they have been in China until at least recent times.

Another and exceedingly valuable article of export from Greenland was the white falcon of Baffin Island. Falconry was perhaps the most popular sport in the Middle Ages and the white falcon was the most highly esteemed of all hunting birds.[24] The kings of Norway early reserved these birds for themselves and used them as diplomatic instruments when they wished to gain the good will of other sovereigns. Thus King Hakon Hakonarson gave some to Henry III of England and to other potentates.[25] Legends on medieval maps identify the Arctic archipelago of Canada as the islands from which falcons come.[26]

More exotic, rarer, and more valuable were live polar bears. These may be called the darlings of medieval kings. Henry III of England had one, a gift from King Hakon Hakonarson, which was allowed to fish daily in the Thames. Emperor Frederick II gave one, which he no doubt obtained from Hakon Hakonarson, to Sultan El. Kamil. These exotic animals were trapped by the Green-

turhistorisk Leksikon for nordisk Middelalder (Copenhagen, 1956—), I, 462–463; *Diplomátarium Islandicum* (Copenhagen and Reykjavik, 1857—), II, 235–236; *Grönlands historiske Mindesmaerker*, III, 48, 244.

[22] *Diplomatarium Norvegicum* (Oslo, 1915—), XIX, 191–192.

[23] Paul Nörlund, *Norse Ruins at Gardar*, Meddelelser om Grönland, LXXVI, No. 1 (Copenhagen, 1930).

[24] On falconry see Bjorn Pordarson, *Íslenzkir falkar*, Safn til sögu Íslands, Sec. Ser. I, 5 (Reykjavik, 1957).

[25] *Diplomátarium Islandicum*, X, 2, 4. Cf. *Flateyjarbok* (Christiania, 1860–1868), III, 117–118, 197.

[26] For example, on the Catalan world map in the Biblioteca Estens in Modena of 1350 and on Martin Behaim's globe of 1492.

landers in northern Greenland and in the Canadian Arctic where ruins of their bear traps are still to be found.[27]

Whether the Greenlanders exported the down of the eider duck is not known. They did, however, construct nests and lay out nesting grounds for the duck in Greenland, Baffin Island, and other islands much further north.[28]

The coarse woollen cloth known as wadmal which was an article of export from Iceland may also have been exported from Greenland. The furs of the Arctic fox and caribou hides are other possible exports.

The above-mentioned riches of these Arctic lands and waters, together with unlimited quantities of fish and seals, proved an irresistible magnet to many of the inhabitants of Greenland. From the very beginning hunting was an important supplement to husbandry in the economy of the immigrants. Very early some of them moved out of the farming settlements and concentrated on hunting in various parts of the region which came to be known as Nordrseta, i.e., northern Greenland and the eastern Canadian Arctic, including Labrador and the shores of Hudson Bay.[29] They adopted, in other words, what we would call an Eskimo way of life and they are to be identified with the people known as Tunnit in the legends of the Eskimos.

The Eskimo tradition is that the Tunnit "were a gigantic race formerly inhabiting the northeastern coast of Labrador, Hudson Strait, and southern Baffin Island. Ruins of old stone houses and graves, which are ascribed to them by the present Eskimo, are found throughout this entire section. . . . Briefly we may say that there is evidence, archaeological as well as traditional, that the Tunnit formerly inhabited both sides of Hudson Strait." [30]

It has of course been vigorously denied that the Tunnit were

[27] T. J. Oleson, "Polar Bears in the Middle Ages," *Canadian Historical Review,* XXXI (1950), 47–55, and the works there cited.

[28] G. and F. Isachsen, "Hvor langt mot nord kom de norrøne Grønlendinger," *Norsk Geografisk Tidsskrift,* IV (1932), pp. 75–78; Duason, *Landkönnun,* pp. 812–827.

[29] Isachsen, "Hvor langt mot nord," pp. 75–92; Duason, *Landkönnun,* pp. 427–455.

[30] E. W. Hawkes, *The Labrador Eskimo* (Ottawa, 1916), pp. 143–150.

Icelanders and the subject has been surrounded by an air of mystery. They have been identified as just another Eskimo tribe, as North American Indians, and recently as the bearers of the so-called Dorset Culture[31] (discussed below). All of these identifications must be rejected. In the legends the Tunnit are carefully distinguished from the Eskimos, the Indians are well known, and the description of the Tunnit cannot possibly fit them. The Dorset people were in these regions hundreds of years before the Tunnit and are indeed in Eskimo legends described in terms which make it impossible to identify them either with the Tunnit or with the Eskimos. The only people who answer the description given of the Tunnit in the legends are the Icelandic settlers of Greenland — and their descendants, who, abandoning husbandry, moved out of the farming settlements and became hunters in the "great north."

When the Icelanders came to Greenland they found no inhabitants in the part they settled and explored, but they did find relics of a people which reminded them, says the twelfth-century chronicler,[32] of the people they were to meet in Vinland a few years later and whom they called the Skraelings, a word which means wizened or shriveled. Now at this time there were in the eastern Canadian Arctic and in Labrador no other people than the so-called Dorset Eskimos. Previous to 1925 their existence was virtually unknown. The eminent Canadian anthropologist Diamond Jenness, on the basis of artifacts collected by Eskimos at Cape Dorset or the southwest coast of Baffin Island and on Coats Island, was able through a brilliant piece of detective work to identify them as belonging to a distinct and hitherto unknown culture.[33] (Incidentally this was a repetition of Jenness' earlier interpretation of the old Bering Sea culture which he made in the same way on the basis of a number of artifacts.) Since then other Dorset culture

[31] Duason, *Landkönnun*, pp. 736–767; J. Meldgaard, "Dorset Kulturen," *Kuml*, 1955, pp. 171, 176.

[32] Ari Þorgilsson, *Íslendingabók*, ed. H. Hermannsson, Islandica XX (Ithaca, N.Y., 1930), Ch. 6.

[33] Diamond Jenness, "A New Eskimo Culture in Hudson Bay," *Geographical Review*, XV (1925), 428–437.

sites have been found as far south as Newfoundland and as far north as northwest Greenland and Ellesmere Island.[34] Outside of some Indians which the Icelanders might have met on Newfoundland or the eastern coast of the United States, the bearers of the Dorset Culture are the only people whom the Icelanders in Greenland can have met on the hunting expeditions which they made from the farming settlements to the various lands lying north, south, and west. The arrival of the Dorset people in the eastern Arctic — and whence they came nobody knows — has been variously dated, but a reasonable date would seem to be about 500 B.C. and as a distinct culture the Dorset disappears in the eleventh and twelfth centuries, i.e., shortly after the coming of the Vikings.

There then appears a new culture in Greenland and the eastern Canadian Arctic which was first identified in 1922 and 1923 as such by Therkel Mathiassen, the distinguished Danish archaeologist on the Fifth Thule Expedition.[35] The principal sites he investigated were at Chesterfield Inlet, Melville Peninsula, Southampton Island, northern Baffin Island, and King William Island. Since then Thule Culture sites have been discovered from Greenland in the east to Siberia in the west.[36]

The Thule Culture is regarded by most scholars as having originated in Alaska, gradually spreading eastward across the Canadian Arctic to Greenland. Evidence in support of this view has, however, not been forthcoming and there are serious objections to it. The oldest Thule Culture sites so far discovered are in Greenland and the youngest in Alaska — a fact which has forced those who believe in the eastward progress of the culture to postulate a return movement westward in the last two or three centuries.[37]

[34] William E. Taylor, "Review and Assessment of the Dorset Problem," *Anthropologica*, n.s. I (1959), 1–23.

[35] Therkel Mathiassen, *Archaeology of the Central Eskimos*, Report of the Fifth Thule Expedition 1921–24, IV (Copenhagen, 1927).

[36] William E. Taylor, Jr., "Hypotheses on the Origin of Canadian Thule Culture," *American Antiquity*, XXVIII (1963), 456–464.

[37] J. Alden Mason, "Excavations of Eskimo Thule Culture Sites at Point Barrow, Alaska," *Proceedings of the 23rd International Congress of Americanists* (New York, 1930); Henry B. Collins, "The Origin and Antiquity of the Eskimo," Smithsonian Institution Annual Report, 1950 (Washington, D.C., 1951), pp. 426–427.

Therkel Mathiassen also notes that "the art of the Thule Culture manifests a steady degeneration gradually as it spreads from Alaska eastwards." [38] This strange fact is difficult to explain. Even stranger is the fact that the excavation of the oldest known Thule sites, those in Greenland, which have been assigned to the eleventh or twelfth century, reveals that the Thule Culture already at that time was not a stone age culture but an iron age culture.[39]

How are these things to be explained? It must be said that if we accept the hypothesis that the Thule Culture originated in western America explanation is difficult if not impossible. If, on the other hand, we accept the opposite hypothesis that the Thule Culture originated in Greenland and gradually moved westward many pieces fall into place. The great drawback of so much Eskimo research is that it has been studied in a historical vacuum. But what was the historical situation in Greenland and the Arctic in, say, the eleventh and twelfth centuries? There were at that time in southern Greenland the descendants of the Vikings who had settled Greenland in the last years of the tenth century and who had been increasingly spreading to various parts of the Arctic outside the farming settlements of southwest Greenland. Here they could encounter only one other people — the so-called Dorset Eskimos. The Vikings had iron tools and weapons, at least to a considerable extent. They were skilled in the hunting of sea and land mammals. The Dorset people were, to judge from all medieval descriptions of them, an extremely primitive people, who although they hunted the seal, walrus, caribou, polar bear, hares, and foxes and some whales did not hunt the narwhal, beluga, or right whale. They had no dogs and consequently had only hand sleds. Many of the implements of the Thule Culture are not to be found among the Dorset.[40] And it is suddenly in the eleventh century that we find the Thule Culture, with iron implements, dogs and dog sleds, its members skilled in the hunting of the narwhal, beluga, and the right whale, and possessing various implements lacking in the Dorset

[38] Mathiassen, *Archaeology of the Central Eskimos.*

[39] Henry B. Collins, "Recent Developments in the Dorset Culture Area," *American Antiquity*, XVIII (1953), 34–35.

[40] Cf. Collins, "The Origin and Antiquity of the Eskimo," pp. 426–428.

Culture, all this at sites where it can be shown that the two existed for a time contemporaneously.

I have elsewhere[41] attempted to trace the evidence which points to an early intermixture between the Dorset people and the Tunnit, i.e., the Icelanders who left the farming settlements and adopted what we would call an Eskimo way of life. At the time they left the settlements they possessed iron implements and were able, possibly for some decades, to replace these with fresh iron acquired through trade with the expeditions the farmers are said to have sent annually to the rich hunting grounds north and west of their farms. However, as gradually the supply of iron grew less they had to resort to the manufacture and use of bone and stone weapons. Thus as these intermingled stone and iron age people moved westward, the crude weapons which resulted from the inexperience of an iron age people in working bone and stone would gradually grow refined and have attained a high quality by the time Alaska was reached.

Just as the Icelanders moved northwest and south from Greenland, the Dorset people moved south along the west coast of Greenland and by 1266 they had, it would seem, almost reached the northern region of the Western Settlement. Skeletal remains from the Western Settlement dating about 1300 show that the intermixture of the Vikings and the Skraelings had begun in the Western Settlement itself,[42] and in 1342, according to Icelandic annals, the descendants of the Vikings there departed en masse for regions unknown.[43] The Eastern Settlement managed to avoid this same fate until the beginning of the sixteenth century.

Racial intermixture is now accepted by the majority of scholars as the most reasonable explanation for the extinction of the Icelandic language and the Christian religion in the farming settlements of Greenland and the abandonment of the farms which were

[41] In my forthcoming Volume I of the Canadian Centenary Series which covers the years 880–1632 of Canadian history.

[42] Cf. K. Fischer-Moller, *The Mediaeval Norse Settlements in Greenland*, Meddelelser om Grönland, LXXXIX, No. 2 (Copenhagen, 1942), 78–82.

[43] Gisli Oddsson, *Annalium in Islandia Farrago*, ed. H. Hermannsson, Islandica X (Ithaca, N.Y.: 1917), p. 2.

established there at the end of the tenth century. But some of the older theories about the disappearance of the settlements die hard and new ones appear. Among the former is the belief that the puny Skraelings in a bloody war exterminated the descendants of the hardy Vikings. This view is maintained in the face of a complete lack of evidence for any such warfare. Malnutrition and consanguineous marriages are two explanations advanced to account for an entirely unfounded belief in the physical degeneration of the Icelanders in Greenland. A number of scholars believe that there was a deleterious change in the climate of Greenland in the fourteenth and fifteenth centuries, but the evidence for this seems at present inadequate. That the settlements were wiped out by epidemics and plagues is a theory supported by little evidence, as is the view that the worms of a butterfly so thoroughly destroyed all vegetation that husbandry became impossible.[44]

There is no escaping the conclusion that racial intermixture accounts for the disappearance of the Icelandic colonies in Greenland. This, however, immediately raises the question: Where is the product of this racial intermixture which we know to have begun at least as early as the thirteenth century?[45] There can be only one answer: the Thule Culture and its descendants, the present-day Eskimo of Greenland and the eastern Canadian Arctic. The Thule Culture begins with an iron age people as the dominant partner but gradually as time passes the more primitive partner gains the ascendancy and the European culture and language of the formerly dominant people are submerged and virtually disappear.

We have come a far distance from the eighth and ninth centuries when the Vikings left the shores of Norway and Denmark and made their way not only to almost all parts of Europe but also to many parts of the Western Hemisphere. It is their fate in the Arctic regions that I have attempted to trace — a less well known

[44] The various theories are discussed at length (with much bibliographical information) by Corrado Gini, "Sulla scomparsa delle colonie normanne in Graenlandia," *Genus*, XIII (1957), 62–131.

[45] Cf. Fischer-Moller, *The Mediaeval Norse Settlements in Greenland*, pp. 78–82.

chapter than many in the history of these intrepid navigators and colonizers.

The Vikings were indeed bold, courageous, and daring individualists but they had another trait equally important. They were among the most assimilable people in history. The Swedish Vikings went to Russia and within a century or two had lost their language and religion and were almost indistinguishable from the people among whom they had settled and whom they ruled. Norwegian and Danish Vikings met the same fate in the British Isles, France, and southern Italy. In the process of assimilation they did make great contributions in many fields in all these countries, but they lost their distinctive identity and in some cases became, so to speak, "more Roman than the Romans." In all these cases, however, they were meeting and being absorbed into cultures at least as well developed as their own and in some cases more highly developed. In Greenland and the Canadian Arctic, where the process is the same — intermixture with the native population with a consequent loss of language and religion — there is only the difference that the culture met with was an extremely primitive one, which the Vikings then raised to one of the most viable in the world under the conditions encountered in its habitat. In this process, however, their original culture suffered a deterioration. But all was not lost. The end product was a people who have no peers in geniality, good humor, cheerfulness in adversity, and lack of bellicosity. The world could do with more of them.

) KARL F. MORRISON (

THE CHURCH, REFORM, AND RENAISSANCE
IN THE EARLY MIDDLE AGES

EARLY in the fourteenth century, Petrarch, a noted antiquary and a poet of sorts, wrote patronizingly of medieval scholars. Theirs had been a world of darkness, he said, in which only a few men of genius had prevailed over contemporary error to glimpse the truth; and even these men had seen through a glass darkly.[1] Petrarch wrote with the easy disdain of the classicist toward those who are not conversant with the languages and the literatures of Greece and Rome, and with the pride of a man who felt that the revival of classical studies to which he himself contributed had exalted his day over more benighted ages. This condescending spirit has persisted. For all his elegance and wit, Professor Highet does nothing but repeat opinions more than half a millennium old when he writes: "The sense of beauty always exists in mankind. During the Dark Ages it was almost drowned in blood and storms; it reappeared in the Middle Ages, although hampered and misdirected. Its revivification as a critical and creative faculty in the Renaissance was one of the greatest achievements of the spirit of Greece

[1] See T. E. Mommsen, "Petrarch's Conception of the 'Dark Ages,'" in E. F. Rice, Jr., ed., *Medieval and Renaissance Studies* (Ithaca, N.Y., 1959), p. 106.

143

and Rome." [2] And again: "The Dark Ages in western Europe were scarcely civilized at all. Here and there, there were great men, noble institutions, beautiful and learned works; but the mass of people were helpless both against nature and against their oppressors. . . . The very physical aspect of Europe was repellent . . . the land and natives were nearly as savage as in central Africa. In contrast to that gloomy and almost static barbarism, the Middle Ages represent the gradual, steady, laborious progress of civilization; and the Renaissance a sudden explosive expansion, in which the frontiers of space and time and thought were broken down or pushed outwards with bewildering and intoxicating speed." [3]

Stung by this sort of judgment, medievalists have laboriously tallied references to Cicero and Virgil, reconstructed curricula of instruction, and registered any outbursts of what Highet calls the "sense of beauty," seeking to establish as fact that the humane spirit, the knowledge and admiration of the classics, and the secularism of the Renaissance were present in the early Middle Ages. This has led to a confusing proliferation of renaissances. Almost every century can now boast a classical revival. Even in sixth-century Gaul, where books were few and readers fewer, one king (Chilperic, the grandson of Clovis) attempted to facilitate writing by adding four letters to the alphabet, encouraged the purification of texts, and expressed his own cultural pretensions by having a statue carved representing himself as the sun-god Apollo bearing his lyre before him.[4]

These studies have served a useful purpose in showing clearly that classical authors were read and appreciated throughout the early Middle Ages. But the term "renaissance" has become virtually meaningless through very frequent and general usage. Indeed, its indiscriminate application to cultural movements in that period was never well advised or appropriate for one critical reason. That is, it leaves out of consideration the goals of the movements, the purposes for which study of the classics was cultivated. Pe-

[2] G. Highet, *The Classical Tradition* (New York, 1957), p. 21.
[3] *Ibid.*, p. 11.
[4] H. Waddell, *The Wandering Scholars* (New York, 1955), p. 25.

trarch and the other leaders of the Italian Renaissance cultivated classical learning for its own sake. A pride in the achievements of their ancestors and a desire to revive the spirit of past greatness in their own time led them to study the known literary and artistic works of antiquity and to ransack libraries and to excavate ancient sites in search of hidden works. Every ancient artifact, every ancient poem or history, was an expression of the spirit of the past; through possession of the artifact and study of the literary work, the fourteenth-century Italian humanists sought to capture and to share in the spirit of Imperial Rome.

Leaders in the earlier "renaissances" were not Italians, and consequently they were not impelled by the strong Roman or Italic patriotism which motivated Petrarch and his contemporaries. They did not cultivate classical studies because the works read had some intrinsic value, but rather because study of ancient authorities was thought likely to serve some specific and predetermined ends. The revival of classical learning was not an end in itself; instead, it was merely a part of a broader program. Finally, even though they read Horace and Virgil with pleasure, the earlier scholars sought their inspiration, not in pagan antiquity, but in Christian Rome.

The focus of the Carolingian and Ottonian renaissances was theological, and the learned apparatus of the seven liberal arts and classical scholarship was subordinated to the understanding of the Scriptures. The greatest works of the Carolingian movement — the Alcuinian Rescension of the Scriptures, the revised order of liturgical service, and the learned treatises of John Scotus Erigena and Hincmar of Rheims — all treat of strictly theological or, more broadly, ecclesiastical problems. Alcuin himself, whom Einhard calls "the most learned man of his time," the presiding genius of the Carolingian Renaissance, described this characteristic explicitly when he compared the learning of antiquity with the learning of his own day. He congratulates Charlemagne for encouraging intellectual activity: "Your intentions have so far prevailed that a new Athens is taking shape in Francia, or, so to speak, an Athens more lovely than the ancient one. For ennobled by the teaching of Christ, our wisdom surpasses all the wisdom of the Academy. The ancient Athens had only the disciples of Plato to instruct her; but still, formed by the seven liberal arts, her glory has not ceased to shine. Our wisdom, however, is endowed beyond this with the seven-fold fullness of the Spirit, and exceeds all the dignity of worldly wisdom." [5] A century and one-half later, when Otto I undertook the encouragement of learning, he patterned his own patronage on that of Charlemagne and adopted the theological stamp of the earlier movement. In Ottonian Germany as in Caroline Gaul, the royal court and the greater ecclesiastical and secular princes maintained schools where the ancient Roman curriculum of the arts was taught, and in some of these foundations, Greek — a language which even Petrarch never mastered — was taught. But these schools existed, in the main, for the training of clergy, and, as the biographies of numerous bishops of the Ottonian period show, the seven liberal arts were taught to prepare the future clergy, especially the higher clergy, for interpreting the Scriptures and administering Church property. (Toward the middle of the eleventh century, Wipo complained vigorously that in Germany no one received instruction unless he were a cleric.[6]) Finally, on the eve of the renaissance of the twelfth century, a distinguished ecclesiastic gave his judgment on the relative values of the classics and Holy Writ: "Once was Cicero music in my ears, the songs of the poets beguiled me, the philosophers shone upon me with golden phrases, the sirens enchanted my soul nigh unto death. The Law and the Prophets, Gospel and Epistle, the whole glorious speech of Christ and His servants, seemed to me a poor thing and empty. I know not what the son of Jesse whispered in my ear, so gracious in its consonance of speech and thought, that all these others whom I once had loved fell inarticulate and silent." [7]

The leaders of the cultural revivals in the ninth, tenth, and late

[5] Ep. 170, MGH Epp. K. A. II, p. 270.
[6] *Tetralogus*, v. 197ff, in H. Bresslau, ed., *Die Werke Wipos*, 3rd ed. (Hanover, 1919), p. 81.
[7] Peter Damian, Sermo LXII, Migne PL. 144, 852. The translation is Miss Waddell's in *The Wandering Scholars*, p. 91.

eleventh centuries reiterate the thought that they are engaged in a work of restoration, a work in which the remains of antiquity are useful instruments. But when Charlemagne built his new capital at Aachen and called it "the second Rome," he referred not to the pagan Rome of Julius Caesar or Augustus, but to the Christian Rome of Constantine or Theodosius the Great.[8] Students labored in the liberal arts, not to capture the spirit of a glorious past, but to acquire administrative skills useful to the Church and to the king. In temper and in goals, the so-called "renaissances" of the early Middle Ages were quite alien to the Italian Renaissance of the fourteenth century, so alien in fact that the term "renaissance" should not be applied to them at all.

Recently, scholars have given some attention to this problem of nomenclature. Some of them have washed their hands of the whole business by asserting that there were no renaissances in the early Middle Ages. They leave the matter there, without telling us what we should properly call the unnamed movements. Others have proposed the terms "renascence" or "proto-renaissance,"[9] but these terms preserve the classics-centered connotations which must be avoided. Like the word "renaissance," they cast the nature of the movements in question and their contributions to cultural development into false perspective, for they emphasize the revival of classical studies, an important ancillary aspect of those movements, but not their principal goal.

These early cultural revivals were only parts of greater movements which had as their first purpose the encouragement of Scriptural study and the purging of error from theological doctrines and of corruption from the administration of the Church. Charlemagne encouraged the study of Latin, and consequently the study of

[8] See especially R. Krautheimer, "The Carolingian Revival of Early Christian Architecture," *Art Bulletin*, XXIV (1942), 1–38.

[9] See the fine essay by E. Panofsky, "Renaissance and Renascences," *Kenyon Review*, VI (1944), 201–236, fully developed in his *Renaissance and Renascences in Western Art*, 2 vols. (Stockholm, 1960), and the comments upon the article by U. T. Holmes, Jr., "The Idea of a Twelfth-Century Renaissance," *Speculum*, XXVI (1951), 642–651, W. A. Nitze, "The So-Called Twelfth Century Renaissance," *Speculum*, XXIII (1948), 464–471, and E. M. Sanford, "The Twelfth Century — Renaissance or Proto-Renaissance?" *Speculum*, XXVI (1951), 635–642.

classical authors, expressly because, as he himself wrote, "we have begun to fear lest, just as the monks appear to have lost the art of writing, so also they may have lost the ability to understand the Holy Scriptures; and we all know that, though mistakes in words are dangerous, mistakes in understanding are still more so. Therefore, we urge you to be diligent in the pursuit of learning and to strive with humble and devout minds to understand more fully the mysteries of the Holy Scriptures." [10] Facility in Latin, acquired through the study of classical authors, was merely the key which opened the understanding of the Scriptures, which led to close scrutiny of the writings of the Fathers and to exact knowledge of the laws of the early Church. The so-called "renaissances" of the early Middle Ages are more properly called "reforms," or aspects of "reforms," not because they were lacking in humane disciplines, nor because the classical authors were unknown or unappreciated, but because of the purposes they served. "Renaissance" is a basically secular concept; "reform" is its ecclesiastical counterpart. Both reject the immediate past as being corrupt, and attempt to improve or overturn deficient institutions, practices, and opinions by returning to the standards of older and better ages. Consequently, both encourage learning; for since the standards of the past lie in the writings of the past, they can be discovered only by research and study. If, as in the case of the fourteenth century and of the earlier movements, the standards are sought in antiquity, such work involves mastery of the classical languages. Both are, in short, intellectual revolutions. When he wrote disparagingly of medieval scholars, Petrarch spoke for the revolutionaries of the Renaissance. The revolutionaries of all the early reforms had their spokesman in a pope of the eleventh century, Gregory VII, when he wrote that he would not allow the reform which he led to be obstructed by custom, "for it must be observed that the Lord says, 'I am the Truth and the Life' [cf. John 14:6]. He does not say, 'I am custom,' but rather, 'I am the Truth.' And surely, to use the statement of St. Cyprian, any custom — however old, however

[10] MGH Cap. Reg. Fr. I, no. 29, p. 79.

148

common — must be entirely subordinated to Truth, and the practice which is contrary to Truth must be abolished." [11]

Judged by the criteria of classical scholarship, the cultural movements, the reforms of the early Middle Ages, deserve the strictures which classicists have issued against them since the time of Petrarch. The sense of truth to which Gregory VII referred — the search for theological verities and the attempt to implement those verities in the administration of the Church — is very different from the "sense of beauty" which Professor Highet seeks and which he finds deficient in medieval Europe. And yet it is harsh to censure an age distinguished for its advances in legal thought and institutional development and for its artistic productions as a period of "gloomy and almost static barbarism" simply because it does not meet standards arbitrarily imposed upon it by later critics. Every age must be judged according to its own standards, and according to the positive contributions it makes to the progress of civilization. By the standards of the early Middle Ages, revivals of classical learning accompanied and were later encompassed by reform of the Church; in serving these standards, the age made distinctive and important contributions to European culture in the revival of law and theology, and in the development of political theory. Its greatest direct achievement was in ecclesiology.

The scrutiny of Christian antiquity, of which the classical revivals were a part, posed two questions: "What is the Church?" and "How is the Church rightly to be governed?" In answering these questions, medieval scholars dramatically changed the concept of the Church as an institution in this world: they formulated doctrines which could be called "juristic ecclesiology." Because the questions which they were trying to answer required a definition of what could be accepted as authentic law in the Church, scholars were at great pains to study the canons of councils, the letters of bishops, the writings of the Fathers, papal decretals, and

[11] G. B. Ladner, "Two Gregorian Letters on the Sources and Nature of Gregory VII's Reform Ideology," *Studi Gregoriani*, V (1956), 225ff, and H. G. Krause, *Das Papstwahldekret von 1059 und seine Rolle im Investiturstreit* (published as *Studi Gregoriani*, VII [1960]), p. 39.

secular laws to decide which were the most authoritative. Because their questions required specification of the lines of authority in the Church, they had to define more precisely than earlier thinkers the relative powers of bishops, archbishops, and popes; and, most important, they had to establish where supreme authority in the Church rested. There was no unanimity in the legal and administrative theories which this work produced. Two answers predominated. The first was the conciliar theory, which held that supreme authority rested in general councils, and that only such councils could establish law in the Church and judge all bishops. The second was the doctrine of Petrine primacy, according to which the bishop of Rome held final authority in the Church, establishing laws and exercising disciplinary powers over all clergy and even over general councils. Out of the conflicts between these two theories came doctrines which were of the greatest importance to later political thought outside the ecclesiastical context: the conflicting doctrines of monarchy, popular sovereignty, and representative government.

There is very little juristic ecclesiology in the Fathers. Christian antiquity, to which medieval authors looked for inspiration, was rich in theology, but poor in the precise legal definitions which they sought. It is true that St. Jerome affirms very strongly the supremacy of the bishop of Rome in matters of faith,[12] and that St. Augustine maintains just as strongly that supreme authority rests in the episcopacy as a whole and, therefore, in general councils.[13] These Fathers, who, at one time, entertained as cordial a distaste for each other as they could within the limits of Christian charity, did not elaborate upon their contradictory theses. They never discussed in detail the bases and nature of authority, and the limits of rightful government in the Church. Indeed, they neglected the primary questions which would have led to a discussion of these problems: nowhere do the Fathers distinguish the clergy as an order subject to a law other than the one to which laymen

[12] Ep. 15, 1, 2; ep. 16, 2. See E. Caspar, *Geschichte des Papsttums*, I (Tübingen, 1930), 246.

[13] Ep. 53, 2; Retractationes I, 21, 1. See Caspar, *Geschichte des Papsttums*, I, 338–339.

were subject, and nowhere do they give a clear formulation of what constituted ecclesiastical law. Despite these major deficiencies, the patristic age made two contributions to later juristic thought concerning the Church. The first was the practice of taking important matters, such as questions of faith and the trials of bishops, before synods and councils. And the second was the image of the Church as the body of Christ, a spiritual community living in the world, but being independent of the governments and laws of the world. These points of synodal or conciliar procedure and the independence of the Church were central to the development of more sophisticated legal doctrines; but, in the age of the Fathers, the Church was not yet considered a predominantly legal institution, and St. Augustine's statement that the "Church is the congregation of the faithful" had only mystical or theological connotations.

The theological concept of the Church as formulated by the Fathers became a permanent and basic part of ecclesiological thought. But the structure of that thought was incomplete as it stood without reference to the administrative side of the Church. Scholars are agreed — from Mirbt to Merzbacher[14] — that the first major step in supplying this deficiency came in the eleventh century.

As in many cases of scholarly agreement, this consensus is inadequate. Two hundred years earlier, the Frankish clergy formulated juristic ecclesiology of remarkable sophistication. In attempting to revive the spirit of Christian antiquity, the Carolingian reform purified Scriptural texts, reformed the liturgy, received for the first time the complete body of the canons of early Church councils, recovered some elements of Roman law, and collected papal decretals in a convenient and systematic form. Fed by all

---

[14] R. Seeberg, *Der Begriff der christlichen Kirche, I. Teil: Studien zur Geschichte des Begriffes der Kirche* (Erlangen, 1885), p. 59. A. L. Mayer, "Das Kirchenbild des späten Mittelalters und seine Beziehungen zur Liturgiegeschichte," in A. Mayer, ed., *Vom christlichen Mysterium: Gesammelte Arbeiten zum Gedächtnis von Odo Casel, O.S.B.* (Düsseldorf, 1951), p. 277. F. Merzbacher, "Wandlungen des Kirchenbegriffes im Spätmittelalter: Grundzüge der Ekklesiologie des ausgehenden 13., des 14. und 15. Jahrhunderts," *Zeitschrift fuer Rechtsgeschichte*, K. A., LXX (1953), 275. C. Mirbt, *Die Publizistik im Zeitalter Gregors VII.* (Leipzig, 1894), p. 551.

this, the Carolingian clergy went beyond the largely theological ecclesiology of the age they sought to imitate. Approaching the very questions which the Fathers neglected, they attempted to set the clergy apart from laymen as being under a law of their own, and to define precisely the components of ecclesiastical law.[15]

For the first time in the history of the western Church, the doctrines of papal supremacy and conciliarism were juxtaposed in terms of law. The advocates of the papal monarchy argued that, since Christ had said to St. Peter, "Thou art Peter, and upon this rock I will build my Church, and the gates of Hell shall not prevail against it" (Matthew 16:18), St. Peter had become the principal representative of Christ in the Church, and that, just as St. Peter was set above the other Apostles, so was his successor, the bishop of Rome, set above all other bishops. They held that only the bishop of Rome could establish law in the Church, and that his decretals were consequently "canons." They argued that no conciliar or synodal decrees had legal validity without the approval of the pope, and further that no synods or councils could meet without being called by him. Those who questioned these doctrines they condemned as "blasphemers against the Holy Spirit."[16]

The thinkers who upheld the supremacy of the General Council protested that Christ had spoken to St. Peter merely as the representative of the other Apostles, and that whatever powers had been given to St. Peter had been given to the other Apostles as well. All the Apostles alike had been given the gift of the Holy Spirit; and all their successors, the bishops, had likewise received it in the episcopal consecration. All bishops held the same powers; therefore, no bishop was superior in authority to any other. Consequently, the conciliarists argued, supreme authority in the Church did not belong to one bishop, but rather to all bishops; and it was exercised through assemblies of bishops, or councils. Their argument is the reverse of the papal supremist position, for they

[15] For a fuller exposition of this argument, see my study, *The Two Kingdoms: Ecclesiology in Carolingian Political Thought* (Princeton, N.J., 1964).

[16] F. Maassen, "Eine Rede des Papstes Hadrian II. vom Jahr 869," *Sitzungsberichte der AK. der Wiss. zu Wien*, phil.-hist. Kl., LXXII (1872), 541.

maintained that only conciliar decrees were true law, and that papal decretals had the force of law only when they had been approved by councils.

Both schools accepted the theological implications of St. Augustine's statement that "the Church is the congregation of the faithful," but they had, in their quite different ways, defined the Church in law as well as in theology. Charlemagne's "new Athens," which Alcuin saw marked by wisdom endowed "with the sevenfold fullness of the Spirit, and exceeding all the dignity of worldly wisdom," had sought to recover the spirit and institutions of the early Church; but it had gone far beyond its patristic prototype. Its recovery of Roman and canon law, and its revival of patristic studies, had brought about two new images of the Church, two images of the Church as an institution in this world as well as an eternal City.

The conflict between the monarchical doctrine of papal supremacy and the representative doctrine of conciliarism continued through the Ottonian period and reached its climax in the early Middle Ages in the great reform movement of the eleventh century.

Despite the efforts of reformers in the ninth and tenth centuries, corruption within the Church increased to an appalling degree in the tenth and eleventh centuries. But, from 1046 onwards for nearly a century, the papacy was held by ardent reformers, who were dominated by the desire to purify the doctrine and the administration of the Church, and by the conviction that this could be accomplished only if the reform were led by the Roman Church. Earlier reforms had been led by secular rulers — by Charlemagne and by the Ottos — and the eleventh-century reform itself began with the support of Emperor Henry III. But the reform popes soon separated themselves from imperial control; the earlier reforms had been limited to the territories under the direct control of royal patrons (e.g., Charlemagne could not reform the churches in Mercia), but the papacy, with its claims to universal competence within the Church, extended the reform to every Christian land in the West. This made reform a matter of general concern, and it made the ecclesiological and political doctrines of the reformers the common property of all Christendom.

The greatest of the reform popes, and the one about whom centered the principal controversies of the eleventh-century movement, was Gregory VII. Like his predecessors, Gregory acted according to the lofty claims of papal supremacy. He held that papal decretals were laws in themselves, and that the bishop of Rome, superior to all councils, could overturn the decrees of councils and modify their canons. He was the ruler over all Christians, even over kings. For, as Gregory wrote: "Who does not remember the words of our Lord and Savior Jesus Christ, 'Thou art Peter and on this rock I will build my Church, and the gates of hell shall not prevail against it. And I will give thee the keys of the kingdom of heaven and whatsoever thou shalt bind on earth shall be bound in heaven, and whatsoever thou shalt loose on earth shall be loosed in heaven.' Are kings excepted here? Or are they not of the sheep which the Son of God committed to St. Peter? Who, I ask, thinks himself excluded from this universal grant of the power of binding and loosing to St. Peter unless, perchance, that unhappy man who, being unwilling to bear the yoke of the Lord, subjects himself to the burden of the Devil and refuses to be numbered in the flock of Christ? His wretched liberty shall profit him nothing; for if he shakes off from his proud neck the power divinely granted to Peter, so much the heavier shall it be upon him in the day of judgment." [17]

Gregory's strong implementation of this doctrine aroused resistance and, in some instances, open rebellion among the clergy. Out of this rebellion came three doctrines which undercut the doctrine of Petrine primacy: two of them were, from the first, countertheories — the doctrines of parties opposed to Gregory — but the third Gregory himself encouraged. All were landmarks in the development of doctrines of representative government. The earliest resistance to Gregory's reforms came from the lesser clergy and

[17] Reg. VIII, 21, ed. E. Caspar, *Das Register Gregors VII.* (Berlin, 1920, 1922), p. 547, tr. E. Emerton, *The Correspondence of Pope Gregory VII* (New York, 1932), p. 167.

from the episcopacy in northern Italy, Spain, France, and Germany. His edicts against simony, clerical marriage, and finally lay investiture were calls to battle. In several cities, prelates who read these edicts to their clergy were publicly ridiculed, some were stoned, and others, like the bishop of Brixen, were beaten almost to death. Many bishops refused to enforce the decrees, arguing that Gregory had usurped powers of legislation and powers to determine doctrine which rightly belonged only to general councils, that he had, in fact, contravened the decrees of the Church stated by such councils, and that he had consequently lapsed into heresy and could no longer be considered the true pope. Finally, the German episcopacy, urged on by its king, attempted to enforce the conciliar doctrine: they gathered in council, declared Gregory deposed, and elected another pope. In this deposition, the German bishops had the support of Hugh Candidus, cardinal priest of S. Clemente in Rome, who subscribed the decree of the synod of Brixen (1080) "in the name of all the Roman cardinals."

It was among the cardinals that the second doctrine of resistance developed. The College of Cardinals had come to prominence in the Roman Church only after the reform papacy began its work in the mid-eleventh century, but its powers became very great in a short time. According to the Papal Election Decree of 1059, the cardinals were charged with nominating to the papacy, and it was soon asserted that the cardinal clergy could judge all bishops in the Roman Empire. They were, Peter Damian wrote, "the spiritual senators of the universal Church." [18] In his major decisions, as for example in his decrees against lay investiture and in his excommunications and depositions of Henry IV, Gregory did not consult the lesser cardinal clergy (the cardinal priests and deacons), and in other ways he excluded them from the government of the Church. The reaction of the slighted clergy was strong. Hugh Can-

[18] See especially H. W. Klewitz, "Die Entstehung des Kardinalkollegiums," *Zeitschrift fuer Rechtsgeschichte, K. A.*, XXV (1936), 115–221; S. Kuttner, "Cardinalis: The History of a Canonical Concept," *Traditio*, III (1945), 129–214; and J. Sydow, "Untersuchungen zur kurialen Verwaltungsgeschichte im Zeitalter des Reformpapsttums," *Deutsches Archiv*, XI (1954/5), 18–73.

didus was the first to desert Gregory; in 1084, a year of bitter reversal for the pope, half the College of Cardinals abandoned him, formulating a new doctrine of Church government which gave supreme importance to their own body. For, they argued, the cardinals were the true representatives of the Roman Church, the head of Christendom, and the bishop of Rome was the true pope only so long as the cardinals recognized him as such. Supreme authority rested, according to their position, neither in the general councils nor in the pope alone, but rather in the pope together with the College of Cardinals.

Different as their positions were, the conciliarists and the cardinals could make common cause in opposition to the third doctrine which ultimately subverted the doctrine of Petrine primacy: the doctrine of popular sovereignty in the Church. This position was not clearly formulated, and it is only implied in the letters and actions of Gregory VII himself, the strong defender of papal monarchy. When Gregory discovered that the German bishops had left his decrees against clerical marriage unenforced, he appealed to the laity to abandon the corrupt priests, and laymen responded to this appeal, accusing married clergy and inflicting gross public humiliation upon them. He urged the count of Flanders to expel married priests, and, in case after case, he admonished the laity to withdraw from bishops and lower clergy whom he had judged unworthy of ecclesiastical office. Gregory himself no doubt considered these measures aspects of the pope's immediate government over every Christian. His enemies, however, saw a wider implication, and they argued that, through these measures, the pope had so far dishonored the clergy that laymen no longer obeyed their priests and that they neglected the sacraments. As the German episcopacy wrote in one edict of deposition against him: "The flame of discord which you stirred up through terrible factions in the Roman Church, you spread with raging madness through all the churches of Italy, Germany, Gaul, and Spain. For you have taken from the bishops, so far as you could, all that power which is known to have been divinely conferred upon them through the grace of the Holy Spirit, which works mightily in ordinations.

Through you, all administration of ecclesiastical affairs has been handed over to the madness of the people." [19]

These four doctrines were the results of the attempt to recapture the spirit of Christian antiquity, to revive the Church of the Fathers. Gregory VII himself repeatedly says that he is trying to do nothing other than to restore the ancient canons of the Church to their full vigor, and his enemies affirm just as strongly that they are trying to do the same thing. St. Augustine's image of the Church as the "congregation of the faithful," however, took on a completely new dimension as a result of the reforms of the ninth, tenth, and eleventh centuries. It appeared not simply as a mystical, or sacramental, communion, but equally as a legal body, a corporation, having a specific body of law and precise lines of authority. The "congregation of the faithful" had become a state as well as a church.

And yet, these doctrines had significance far beyond the scope of ecclesiology. It is true that they represent a revolution in the concept of the Church; but the theory of the papal monarchy, the representational theories of the conciliarists and the cardinals, and the nascent doctrine of popular sovereignty continued to develop, and they were later incorporated into doctrines concerning civil government. The papal monarchy corresponded to the later medieval monarchy with its claims to ultimate authority, and many of the same arguments from Roman law which the papalists used in their own defense were used to support the thesis of irresponsible government in temporal kingdoms. The medieval concept of the state as a hierarchy of corporations, each with its own inviolable privileges, derived from the knowledge of Roman law recovered in the eleventh and twelfth centuries; it is closely related to the doctrine of the schismatic cardinals in the time of Gregory VII that the pope, the cardinals, the bishops, the lesser clergy, and the laity, each as a class, had rights which none of the others could infringe. The early Renaissance, or late medieval, theorists Marsilio

[19] C. Erdmann, ed., *Die Briefe Heinrichs IV.* (Leipzig, 1937), p. 66, tr. T. E. Mommsen and K. F. Morrison, *Imperial Lives and Letters of the Eleventh Century* (New York, 1962), p. 148.

of Padua and William of Ockham, with their theories that full sovereignty in State and in Church lay with the commons, were foreshadowed in Gregory's appeal beyond the established organs of Church government to the laity for the execution of his decrees. Parliaments and other representative assemblies of civil states corresponded to Church councils, and the theorists who advocated their supremacy in civil matters found much to support this position in the earlier arguments of the conciliarists.

If the early Middle Ages seem dark, or a period of "gloomy and almost static barbarism" to students of classical learning, it is because they are applying to that age goals and standards which the age itself did not acknowledge or strive after. It is not in the idea of the "Renaissance" that we shall find the proper standards of that period, but rather in the idea of reform; not in the attempt to recover the spirit of pagan antiquity, but rather in the attempt to revive the vigor and the promise of Christian Rome. In this dimension, the early Middle Ages made remarkable contributions to Western civilization, contributions which are present whenever we use the terms "monarchy," "representative government," and "popular sovereignty."

Petrarch did not appreciate the cultural values of the "Dark Ages"; the religious ethos of the period was foreign to him, and he acknowledged judgment under the aspect of time, rather than under the aspect of eternity, as supreme. His older contemporary, Dante, still partook of the earlier spirit. Like men of the early Middle Ages, he honored classical antiquity, but, in his eyes, it did not hold ultimate truth. In the eighth century, Alcuin had written that the learning of Athens was glorious, but that Christian wisdom was yet more glorious, "endowed by the seven-fold fullness of the Spirit." Likewise, in the fourteenth century, Dante received the pagan poet Virgil as his guide through the Inferno and Purgatory on his journey toward divine truth. But Virgil must leave Dante on the threshold of Paradise, the eternal Kingdom, from which he was barred because he had been a pagan. The man whom Dante honored as the greatest poet of classical antiquity could not glimpse the vision of God's eternal glory because he had not been a Christian. Without Virgil, Dante himself continues on his journey into the Heavenly City, and at length he beholds the splendor of Christ enthroned. Rejecting the values of the "renaissance" for those of "reform," he wrote: "O triple Light, which in a single star shining on them their joy can so expand, look down upon this storm wherein we are. If the barbarian . . . seeing Rome and her stupendous works — if he was dazed . . . how dazed past measure must I needs be, I who was come to the divine from man, to the eternal out of time, and from Florence unto a people just and sane." [20]

[20] *Divine Comedy*, tr. L. Binyon, Paradiso XXXI, vv. 28–40.

Index

INDEX